In the Shadow
of the Towers

In the Shadow of the Towers

Collected Works

Edited by Stephanie Izarek and Dan Costa

Writer's Showcase
San Jose New York Lincoln Shanghai

In the Shadow
of the Towers
Collected Works

Writer's Showcase
an imprint of iUniverse, Inc.

For information address:
iUniverse, Inc.
5220 S. 16th St., Suite 200
Lincoln, NE 68512
www.iuniverse.com

Editor: Stephanie Izarek

Cover design by Robert Smith

ISBN: 0-595-24368-1

Printed in the United States of America

To those who lost their lives on September 11, 2001

In a world of destruction one must hold fast to whatever fragments of love are left for sometimes a mosaic can be more beautiful than an unbroken pattern.

—Dawn Powell
The Locusts Have No King

Contents

Acknowledgements

This book was not easy to edit. The content and the sentiment often became overwhelming. But the courage it took for each writer and artist to confront the enormity of the Sept. 11th tragedy and each small "thank you" that accompanied the submissions were reason enough to continue on with the project.

We want to thank each and every person who bravely donated their work to In the Shadow of the Towers—an experiment in creative expression and a true community project—because without them, there would be no book. We also want to thank all our friends and family for their kind words and assurances that this book would be a worthwhile endeavor. We are grateful to Rob Smith for designing an elegant, respectful cover.

Preface

This book was born of the desire to reach out to a community confronted with tragedy and to use creative expression and story sharing as part of the healing process. The works that appear here were generously donated to the project. Any revenue from sales of this book will be given to PS 234, PS/IS 89, and PS 150, in the hopes that it will be put toward art and language program enrichment.

Introduction

In the Shadow of the Towers

The story of September 11th begins on a tragic morning the world will never forget, but it does not end with that day. As the days, weeks, and months followed, a larger story continued to unfold, and this is where our book begins. *In the Shadow of the Towers: Collected Works* is about 9/11, and every day since. It is not one person's story, but rather a collective story. It is a compilation of creative works by our neighbors—writers, poets, artists, mothers, fathers, and children—who have spent a year of their lives grieving, remembering, recovering, and rebuilding after the devastating attacks on our great city, our neighborhood.

It is the story of a community that has thrived in the shadow of towers for the past 30 years and one that will continue to live in a newly cast, unknown shadow for many years to come. It is also about the idea of community—how it has changed because of what we witnessed and the common scar we will all bear for the rest of our lives.

This book is a medium for sharing our personal experiences and perspectives in the spirit of healing and learning. The people of New York, especially residents of Lower Manhattan, whether it be Tribeca, Battery Park City, or the Financial District, now hold a unique place in history: Some were lucky enough to witness the rise of the Twin Towers, but we all saw them fall. *In the Shadow of the Towers* is the voice of these people.

For downtown New Yorkers, 9/11 isn't something framed by a television screen, played in slow motion, and packaged into a titled segment. It was live, and it lingers. As we dropped our children off at school, grabbed a coffee and bagel, and sleepily walked toward the subway on that pristine morning, we watched the first plane fly at absurd speed, low over our heads. We heard the unearthly sound as it crashed into the North Tower. We saw the second plane strike. We felt the panic as we rushed to find our loved ones, the helplessness as we watched others die unimaginable deaths, and the quaking of the streets as both towers fell into an enormous black cloud.

We have smelled the smoke, breathed the ash and metal that covered our homes, choking on the unspeakable. When we were allowed to, we returned home to a place of wild devastation, a place that no longer felt like home. We've looked into our children's fearful eyes when they ask us why, steeled ourselves to reassure them, and have cried silently at the truth.

We were also moved by incredible feats of bravery, as the volunteer rescue workers in their hard hats, the NYPD, the firemen, the National Guard, the EPA, and countless others moved through our neighborhood, their shifts, and fatigue, 24 hours a day. We've listened to the steel remains crash into the barge at Pier 25, formerly our "family-fun" pier, throughout the nights for six months. And we watched from the sidelines the most dedicated of souls dismantle the pile of debris, painstakingly each day, often by hand. Now we stare at the vacant hole, the condemned buildings in their black shrouds, and confront the phantom faces of those lost, posted on random corners, still.

In the works that follow, you will see many common sentiments arise, from the changed meaning of home in Molly Mokros's piece entitled "Home" to the attempt to reconcile New Yorkers' experiences with those outside the city in Carol Mangis's essay "Caught Between Horror and Healing" and Roger Wall's "Identification." And the guilt of survival is ever-present in Sharon Lew Block's email account to family and friends entitled, "Lucky." But one of the most palpable is the consequence of an intense, traumatic sensory experience. For many, the sounds and images of 9/11 have not gone away. We have continued to carry on, caring for our children, doing our jobs, and trying to comfort those around us who may have lost more. Yet, we've had to wrestle with fear each step of the way: Of what has already happened, and to some extent, of what's to come.

As we have tried to heed the advice of well-meaning leaders—"It's time to move on" or "Don't let the terrorists win"—it has often been delivered with haste, without empathy, and rings hollow, especially set against the backdrop of reality: Colleagues, friends, and loved ones are gone. Our neighborhood is wounded. America is at war.

Within this shadow, mundane daily events can take on darker meanings. We hear the roar of jet engines every day, and we look up. We hear the thunder clap of a common summer storm, and we look up. But, as we've come to understand through conversations with downtown residents, we are not alone, and in that—in each neighbor we have leaned on, each familiar face we pass on the street, each teacher who stayed with our children, each business that reopened—there is comfort and strength. This is hope. This is New York.

In this new city, we strive to live, and in every given moment thank God that we have the chance to try. This book is a community's attempt at moving on—but not at the urgings of others or on anyone else's timetable, and certainly not without at least pausing to try to make sense of the senseless, because isn't that the least we can offer to the people whose lives were stolen that day?

And this is why we compiled *In the Shadow of the Towers*. The essays, poems, and art that follow are relevant. They might not be the most heroic or even the most tragic tales, but they are all true in spirit. And they are created with gratitude and the awareness that we have survived.

Some of the contributors have stayed to rebuild, while others are further removed geographically, but everyone who contributed, regardless of location, profession, or age, is very much in touch with the "place."

Interestingly, the submissions themselves changed the direction of the book. When we started this project, we were not looking for stories of "that day." It was more than adequately documented by the media. Television stations broadcast the horrific events live, direct, and with unbearable repetition. Newspapers and magazines printed the dramatic photos and heartbreaking stories of loss and valor. The Internet kept record of every fact and fiction, no matter how obscure, and put it within the reach of anyone with a phone line and a PC.

Everyone in the country, indeed, the world, knew what had happened. The details were all there, so there seemed little point in revisiting it. Our call for manuscripts asked for works dealing with grief, healing, and rebuilding. But when we started reading the manuscripts we saw that one could not exist without the other. What happened on the morning of September 11th was too integral a part of the whole story.

Our hope is that words, poetry and art truly are powerful enough to heal, to comfort, to connect, and yield strength in the midst of adversity. While each story here creates a unique fabric, it is all woven from the same thread: 9/11.

So from our place, in the shadow of the towers, here is our story.

—Stephanie Izarek and Dan Costa

September 10th

Hold on

There is nothing here but time
and the valiant eyes of an infant
unblinking, open wide.

Hold on
remember
your lover's kiss
the last goodnight goodbye
in the fearless space of
summer days, dwindling
the heady hollow promise:
a life war free
only, what self should I be?

Hold on
remember
what was we will always heed
children running in the little league field of green
voices lifted; an echo dancing
through city streets
as familiar as the sea
and we, from the sidelines, appraised
our lucky lives
smiling faces lifted toward the sun
alive in an untainted sky

Remember
the way we walked, then
with innocence
strangely side by side
absurdly confident; absurdly hated
with nothing here but time.

Hold on
did you feel it?
the breeze of ignorance
has fast blown by
the fortune teller turned
the card, secretly
stifling her mournful cry
Hush!
this fate cannot
be reclaimed

Hold on
remember
the simplicity of love of peace,
not to be granted or gambled
stolen or pried from clenched hands
it is
to be cherished
another luxury we can't afford

Remember
the beauty
the privilege
standing tall, a sheath of glistening steel
Brilliant as the steady moon

yet small and fragile, a microscopic truth
only scrutiny could reveal

Hold on
remember
the way we walked,
dear friends,
remember

Hold on

tonight
for dear life
for what follows is
September 11th

—*Stephanie Izarek*

What If?

what if there's
more
than what you
see

what if a
wall
is a secret
door
to a place
you have only
imagined

what if something
happens
that really
shouldn't?
would you
admit it
or forget it?

What would you do?

—*Miles Kaufman*

Miles Kaufman, age 11, is a fifth grade student at PS 234.

This is Not Home

This is Not Home
Bibi Lencek, downtown resident for 21 years, mother of two teenagers,
artist, and art teacher.
(mixed media collage on watercolor paper)

Caught Between Horror and Healing

by Carol Mangis

Over three months have passed since the September 11th terror attacks. Even now, the news is filled with the war in Afghanistan, the hunt for Osama Bin Laden, anthrax, and controversy over how millions of donated dollars will be distributed among victims' families.

In New York, we still share our individual stories of that day with those we haven't seen since before September 11th, and sometimes with strangers we'll never see again. The attacks remain with us; the fear, the disbelief, the outrage, and the sorrow come in waves. Perhaps the intensity has lessened, and we no longer need to talk about it constantly. But there are reminders everywhere—as we pass a firehouse or police station, where candles still burn, fresh bouquets appear, and handwritten "Thank You" and "Our Heroes" posters hang or when we glance downtown and see that hole in our skyline.

Yesterday, I ran into Jack, a friend I hadn't seen in a while and who witnessed the World Trade Center attacks from the roof of his studio's building in the lower East Side. Jack was always pretty big and strong, but now he is 80 pounds lighter—thin and pale. He looks like he never sleeps.

Jack watched the events unfold after the second plane hit, but before the towers came down. He watched as smoke billowed from windows that people smashed open. A man sheltered a woman with his body, whispering courage into her ear. People, bloodied from broken glass, held hands and jumped together, or dived alone.

Jack is a sculptor who works in metal and stone, and has all the tools. He took them to the site and told the authorities that he was in the metalworkers' union. They let him in to help cut steel beams in hopes of rescuing the few survivors. He didn't stop for a couple of days; his ex-girlfriend finally found him in the hospital suffering from exhaustion and smoke inhalation. As Jack told me his story, it seemed he wasn't in the room with us but rather was reliving it all again, for the thousandth time.

I try to take care not to discount the effect of September 11th on Americans who live outside New York and Washington DC. But it does seem that many people are more interested in catching Bin Laden, putting limits on immigration, and curtailing personal freedom in the name of security than they are in dealing with the physical and emotional wounds of the attacks. They wave flags, venerate George W. Bush, fear flying, and worry about the economy. The raw anguish has receded and been replaced by jingoism and a return to enthrallment with celebrities, movies, and TV shows.

About a month ago, I told an out-of-town colleague on the phone that I was feeling sick, like I had a cold, but not exactly. Maybe, I said, it's because of the bad air from the Ground Zero fires. He told me to try echinacea, as if I hadn't said anything about the World Trade Center, or as if it were slightly distasteful to have mentioned it. I imagined him thinking, "Do we really need to talk about that any more?"

I also recently heard from an almost-forgotten friend who found my e-mail address on Classmates.com. She wrote to tell me that her life is wonderful and full, her husband is terrific, and it's great to be in touch with me again. "But you know where I live," I thought. "Why didn't you think to ask me whether I had come through the attacks okay, or say you hoped I hadn't lost someone—a friend, family member, or a lover?"

In New York, I had dreamed that maybe the experience would precipitate a spiritual transformation—a miracle jump to a new level of compassion and understanding for humanity. That seems like a very naïve fantasy now. Even here in New York, where the grief and loss all around us are still so palpable, the coming together, the recognition of commonality, and the simple kindness so many people displayed still exist, but it is definitely muted.

This year, as the holidays approached, I decided to go to Alabama to visit my sister and her family. Though I felt relief even at the thought of going away, I also felt an emotional wrench, because I didn't want to leave the people who could understand my complicated, weird jumpiness and depression—but I went anyway. The trip was long, made longer because I was a random "searchee" at LaGuardia Airport's security checkpoint, and then endured a two-hour delay in Memphis for "mechanical problems."

Although I don't often attend church, it was Christmas Eve and the kids wanted me to go. The ceremony wasn't what I remembered from my own Catholic childhood: a member of the congregation played guitar and people sang Christmas carols and some hymns I didn't recognize. People lifted their arms, as if embracing the air. The pastor then delivered a rather strange sermon—the story of the Christmas Nail, which was new to me—and my mind wandered. I watched my little niece draw on a collection envelope.

Then the pastor asked us to create prayer circles. My sister, her husband, her five children, and I made a circle, and I thoroughly surprised myself by saying, "I have something I want to pray for: My city." We all closed our eyes, and my youngest nephew began to speak. This sweet, normally gawky and blushing 10-year-old boy articulately and compassionately prayed for God to heal New York. I began to cry, and again, I felt that great, limitless sorrow. When we broke the circle, my sister held me, and I felt I might break into sobs—or into pieces. I remembered that there is caring in the world, if you are lucky and know where to find it.

*Carol Mangis is a writer and editor; she has been a New York City resident since 1978 and currently lives in the West Village. This was written in December, 2001 and was originally published at **www.12gauge.com**.*

Towers

Towers, a photograph by Craig Hamrick
Craig Hamrick is an editor and photographer with a studio downtown.
*His work can be seen at **www.craighamrick.com**.*

The Next Plane Out

I watched those planes, those fully fueled bombs
Crash, with annihilation and murder in mind, into
The Twin Towers—the still silhouetted columns of steel.
Those workers at their desks with morning coffee
Having just turned their faces to the glorious late summer sunshine.
Having dropped my own son at daycare, I emerged from depositing
my tax relief check to a sonic boom.
Our relative ease and comforts destroyed: the boarding of a
Jet to return home or satisfy a need for particular elsewheres, leaning
back to
Read within the clouds. Our city, our neighborhood, has captivated
the world while
My home, just blocks from Ground Zero, is blockaded.
Rescue trucks, cranes, secret service, and Con Edison have replaced the
strollers, the children and their nannies, the ice cream truck, free salsa
and easy-listening jazz,
Brian Eno in the Winter Garden.

Each day we wake to still smoldering piles: frail humanity, self-pos-
sessed media, altruistic caregivers. The posters of the missing crinkle in
the rain; collection funds grow. Some friends are fleeing—they must
escape the smoke,
The smell of more troubles in their noses.
Some of us don't know where we can go
What other corners can satisfy our desires?
Where is utter peace and freedom from terror? Is there a field so ver-
dant we can enter its

Embrace, a prayer so total we can surrender to its grace? Should we plow along with
The rescuers, stay and assist our students and our neighbors? Must we get the hell out, pack up the car to find better lives, truer loves, sweeter dignity?

—Cheryl Fish

Cheryl J. Fish is an Associate Professor of English at Borough of Manhattan Community College and lives at Independence Plaza in Tribeca. Her poems and stories have appeared in periodicals and journals, including The Village Voice, New American Writing, Between C&D, *and* Talisman. *She is the editor, with Farah J. Griffin, of the anthology* A Stranger in the Village: Two Centuries of African-American Travel Writing *(Beacon Press, 1999)*

One Story

by Elizabeth Frankenberger

This is not a story about September 11th. It is about every day before September 11th, and every day since. A story about storytelling, about the things we tell ourselves like "Next year things will be better" or "I look ugly in this neckline" or "I'm sure he'll call later." This is a story about the things we say to each other—to our loved ones, our friends, our neighbors. "Next year things will be better" and by the way, "You look pretty in that neckline." "I'll call you later."

It's about a merciless blending of beginnings and endings, day in and day out. The things we said before September 11th, the things we'll say for years to come.

This is not a story about September 11th. It's about me—always me, me, me—and the endless dialogue of dreams and fears lost to the city's din and fray. Oh look, the F-train is coming! It's about reading my horoscope in *Time Out*, pulling up my stockings in public bathrooms, checking my lipstick in the reflection of a telephone booth, stealing toilet paper from the office, popping Advils, eating pizza slices in taxi cabs, writing little notes to strangers. It's a story about Manhattan and myself: The things I do in secret and the places where I hide; the men I don't meet and the women who meet them. The things I was before September 11th, and the things I never will be.

The 6 train is coming. This is what I remember: I was running late, but trying to get to work early. I was on the cross-town bus, heading toward Chelsea Piers. A man listening to his Walkman whispered to me that something terrible had happened at World Trade. We looked down Tenth Avenue and saw the first plume of smoke. We got off the bus. We wished each other luck and said goodbye. Somehow I arrived at my office building, and everyone was on the street, heading for the river, when the second tower was struck.

I called my brother who worked down on Wall Street; my mother in Massachusetts; my father, Michigan; my friends Nina and TMC, midtown; AP and Lisa downtown; and my coworkers dispersed at the piers. No one answered. I lay down on the grass—now sunburned, starving, crying—and continued to dial numbers. Brother, mother. Silence. Brother, mother, Nina. Silence. Then, miraculously, a call. My mother with news of my brother: He got away. He escaped the horror, with ripped pants. He was heading uptown along the East River.

We all have our stories, and this is where I'll end, because mine is not a story about September 11th.

Elizabeth Frankenberger is a copywriter in the book publishing industry. She writes the "Sects and the City" column for KillingtheBuddha.com and is working on a book based on this series.

Hollow Blow

Nothing of consequence said. Action obliterating.
Louder than words. People extinct; about which
one cannot speak, or can but not explain; but
the need to talk about it anyway. The silence
not enough. No respite. Not giving up.

Hands ripping through toppled floors.
Gouging dirt and ash; frantic for their
own dead counterparts. Here, under fire
and smoke, the living meet with their
replicant dead. Carrying them out.
Brother and sister disemboweled.
The voice of reason inside out.
No resurrection here. This tragic
understanding tutankhamuned.

And they say:

Humanity made stronger; we will rise about;
It will show our strength. In this irony,
The eternal irony: the unneedful evil
for the necessary good.

And they say:

To destroy our enemy we must rail.

But the evidence of the ages is stacked
against: to destroy our enemy, we must
destroy our enemies will to destroy;
we must liberate the oppressor as well
as the oppressed. There is ignorance under
one flag, if we consent to it; our humanity
will lie buried there.

But again, easier said. Again just words.

Nothing of consequence with people dead.
No word or phrase of sentence said, can now
assuage or mend, or be put down as grief
so-called reclaim.

—David Hughes

David Hughes is a 31-year-old Irish writer, who has lived in Tribeca with his wife since 1998. He works for the Council on the Environment and continues to write in his spare time.

Aftermath (in pieces)

i

I had read that the moon was at apogee.
Mars would appear bright in the southern sky.
Free from ogreish cloud, it would seem to
form a double star with the star Nunki of the
constellation Sagittarius (The Archer). Tonight
and tomorrow night, Nunki would lie less than
one degree from Mars. Such occultations
apparently, were exceptionally rare. I looked.
It was red for me; that was all. A burnished
flicker, yet profound in spite.

ii

There was talk of coyotes foraging when we heard
this meow. Door open. Windows flung wide. Meat
smokesmearing: In the throes of another last supper.
(The smell must have brought her down?) This puss-puss
mewing. Dainty black and white. Caked with dust from
hillsides. Making her way in. Nose eager.
Purrwappinground.

iii

Hard for us to relax though, out here, even now.
Away from the morgue-siren din of lower Manhattan.
Secure in our Pueblo yet still awhirl. Reliving over and over.
Death and destruction drew us closer, then blew us wide.
To be without home; some glimpse now of other people's lives.
For half a world this a daily. But at least alive. At least alive.

iv

Tumbling. Tumbling. Words reverberate and revive.
That Rabbi in Yankee Stadium, pulpit-stricken, wailing
shofar; those hair-pulling cries. And behind,
multi-denominationals in line. The precepts of every
Great religious tradition binding against:
it's not 3000 that are dead, it's one dead
3000 times. One dead dying over and over for us.
This wordless memory to chastise.

v

From the Quran, Verse 190:

Fight in the path of God those who fight you but do not
Transgress limits. God does not love transgressors.

Transgressors?
Those brothered to you by treaty: women, children, the elderly,
grown men; those who offer peace and a restrained hand.
But all brethren now torn asunder by this, this unholy jihad.
These lunatic imaginings no God an salve. Springs to mind
our own home-grown struggle. Those Troubles on Irish ground.

One and the same. Make no mistake.
No word there to make it blessed doctrine.
It is what it is: blatant violence. Crimes against souls.

vi

Meow. This cat though, Pussinboots, like life itself; a
Liniment outside our wounded whole. *Pasatiempo.*
Ingratiating for a while. Animal in its complete oblivion.
Offering herself up. We too offering our own animal kind.
(The willing osmotics.) Out here under pitchblanket mesa of
starry, starry sky, our life more precious to us and at
once more insignificant: Mars, the moon and Nunki flummoxblind.

vii

Twinkle. Twinkle. Giving ourselves over. Arms intertwined
like exiled lovers: Maria Bonita e Lampiao. Gazing up.
Heavenbound. Waxing lyrical: *how I wonder what they are? Why?*
This light, departed from past distant moments flickershined.
An augur to all that changes; to what endures. Both ascending and
descending towards. Fulcrummed between insipid particle and
spiritwow. A skywatch foisting life-in-death and death-in-life.
All unknowable.
Momentsigh.
The cat tummynuzzling. Life pulsing claw.
The sudden remembered tremors: *Dias de los Muertos* in New York.
(Purrs.)
(Purrs.)
Smiles between us in pieces.
Only half of us here becoming more alive.

—*David Hughes*

Apartment 3S

by Carrie Strauch

Armed with respirator masks, plastic gloves, and scarves for our heads, we walked down Broadway into crowds of milling people and the choking smell of smoke—and death. Susan pulled a shopping cart carrying a new $700 HEPA vacuum cleaner, leading the way to the police barricade near Fulton Street, where we would show our I.D.s and line up with others who needed a police escort in order to access offices or apartment buildings. On any Wednesday morning before September 11th, this part of Broadway would be backed up with city traffic. Today, there were only golf carts transporting police and National Guardsman.

We were going to the place Susan has called home for the last 24 years to take inventory of her apartment for the insurance company. But "home" would be the last word to describe apartment 3S at 125 Cedar Street.

We walked with a policeman along Broadway toward Cedar Street, one block south of the WTC. This was the first time that I would enter "Ground Zero." We came to a 12-foot metal fence covered with green tarp. Another officer let us through and closed the gate behind us.

I tried to keep my focus on Cedar Street, but I was drawn by the sound of heavy machinery and the unexpected expanse of sunlight to my right. I wasn't ready to confront the destruction close up, but we kept walking, quietly—the way you walk when you enter a cemetery to honor the dead.

At the entrance to the blackened, dusty, seemingly abandoned lobby we put on our masks and hoisted the cart up the stairs one step at a time, hesitating often, not just from the physical weight of the cart but also from the psychological weight of what we might encounter in apartment 3S. In my mind the "S" in"3S" always stood for Susan, although it really meant "South," which also means that her life is very different because of this location. Her three kitchen windows faced the Trade Centers, while the others face south onto Cedar Street.

As we opened the door to Susan's apartment, we were overwhelmed. They always say "a picture is worth a thousand words" but here it was more like "ain't nothing like the real thing." Plywood boards now covered the three kitchen windows and blocked out virtually all light, but for one illuminating ray. And then you could see it: Dust. Piled eight inches high, this "dust"—finer and smoother than sand, the consistency of a brownish gray talcum powder—covering everything. There was so much, the air had texture; it was visible. And it began to cling to our skin and clothes like static electricity.

Pieces of matted, crushed, and ripped hunks of paper hurled in from the WTC by the sheer force of the explosion littered the space. Blown-out glass from the windows, the kitchen cabinets, the microwave, picture frames, lamps, and more were all over the floor. Several 3-or 4-foot-long pieces of twisted metal with screws and holes lay amidst more dust, torn papers, and glass shards. More gnarled metal jutted out from the layered piles on the floor.

It was difficult to breathe. As we stood and stared, the fear within became as palpable as the weight of the air. The need to breathe or the fear or something else sent us into sudden motion. With pens and pad in hand, we split up to cover different rooms, but I was glad we were all there together. I opened the kitchen pantry and found more strange dust covering the cans, jars, boxes of cereal, pasta and rice, dog food, liquor, and wine. The brooms, mops, and electric broom would never serve their function again. Nor would the blender, toaster or any other appliance that now had asbestos in their crevices. I found it hard to care about counting cans or objects of value. Yet as awful as it was to go through the apartment, we felt lucky to even have this option.

The open bedroom and living area of Susan and David's loft looked as though it hadn't been cleaned in about 5 years but in contrast to the kitchen, it looked good. The couch, the chairs, the cashmere blanket, all the bed linens and clothes would have to be thrown out. I wondered why we had even brought the HEPA vacuum cleaner today.

From the looks of this, the loft might not be inhabitable for 6 months to a year. Today, Susan isn't even sure if she can live here. How could she know what she wants? This was Susan's home for half of her life, as well as the office for her occupational therapy practice. Within the span of two hours, her home and workspace were gone. But for Susan, who is one to recognize the positive in everything, she is thankful that she, her husband David, and her dogs are alive.

Not sure I wanted to dig down into the unknown just yet, I still had the strong desire to dig through the debris. Iris and Susan felt it, too. I kicked it a bit with my foot, then bent to pick up some papers that must have been in someone's desk or file cabinet. Insurance company charts, investment statements, notes scrawled on a pad from a business meeting, and a ripped presentation cover from AON Corp., and a business card that read Marshall McClenan. Then, a photo of an infant. We all stopped digging.

Soon Iris held up a flat piece of metal she had unearthed and said, "Do you think this is from the plane?" Susan then held up a piece of plastic mat—the kind that secretary's use under their chairs. I put these "artifacts" on top of a bookshelf. I watched them sink into the dust, and I wondered what I would do with them.

The dust haunts me. This pulverized, metallic, silken-smooth powder slips through your fingers, like the ashes of the dead, perhaps. And I wonder who else is here in this room with us?

Susan's neighbor, Andy, then gave me a tour of his place. He pointed out a mangled computer lying in the middle of the room. "It's not mine," he says. There was more metal here—only the pieces were much bigger. More paper, more dust, more debris, more glass and a lot less air. Breathe, I kept repeating to myself. I knew I had to, but the air smelled so bad. I now understood why he just kept walking around and around and around. There wasn't much else to do in this place.

I didn't ask if he was planning to move back in. It's something that you have to see for yourself, as the visual and visceral become interwoven into one big mess inside of you.

Susan wanted to find an old copper box that was important to her and David. She was afraid that it had been stolen because many other things were missing. Various neighbors had reported thefts from their apartments since 9/11 even though the FBI had "set up shop" in Jill's apartment upstairs. And then Susan saw that the window gate to the shaftway was unlocked and the window was open wide. Iris and Susan dug down elbow deep into the dust in search of the box. We were about to call it quits when Susan found it.

After that bit of luck, we thought it time to leave. I caught a glimpse of myself in a mirror that remained in tact. Susan, Iris, and I stood before it, creating a virtual snapshot. There, we three friends stood wearing baseball caps, head coverings, respirator masks, plastic gloves, and clothes covered in dust next to a window boarded up with wood. What's wrong with this picture? And what is right? We were alive, united.

Andy helped Susan put the big chain and lock on the door, placed there by the fire department. We went to the special tent set up specifically designated for "clean up." Men dressed in white protective gear directed us to sinks for hand washing, washed our shoes off with brushes, showed us how to use special machines to rinse our eyes, and then they even put in eye drops. I felt so thankful for these people who spent all day cleaning the shoes of so many people, all with different reasons for being in Ground Zero. I walked out of the tent only to realize that I was right there on the corner of Liberty and Church. Been there a thousand times before September 11th, but now, an enormous void. Negative space. Breathe in. Courage. Breathe out. Fear. Could this open space eventually clear the way for the energy of new ideas or different, endless possibilities? We stood there, hands to hearts, in silence.

Carrie Strauch, a pediatric occupational therapist, energy healer, and writer, is a native New Yorker currently residing in the West Village. (This piece was written in October, 2001.)

Ashes

Everyday, off the subway to the
apartment by the stock exchange, I
breathe the fallen towers and the
bodies turned to dust

if I take them in my lungs
do they continue in my blood?

am I fireman, banker, artist, wife, child?
could I absorb knowledge this way, spirit?

I am three thousand incarnate now; I am New York City now
she baptized me with ash and bonded me through waking nightmares

—*Shelly Reed*

Shelly Reed is a graduate student at New York University, the editor of
Spire Magazine, *and a freelance writer who moved to the financial district
two weeks before 9/11.*

From My Classroom

by Ellen Mullen

On September 11th, I was in my classroom. We were having Morning meeting when Lucy's Mom ran into the classroom. Lucy's Mom said, "The building is falling down! I think she meant to say the Twin Towers were falling down.

Some of the kids in the class started to cry. My friend Audrey was afraid she was not going to be picked up. All of the other parents started coming to the classroom to get their kids.

My Mom came to get me. When we got downstairs by the security guard Angela's desk, my Mom saw my Dad. She was glad to see him. My Mom went with my friend's Mom to use the phone to call her job. After we left P.S. 234, we went to my friend Eve's house in China-town, where we slept over that night. We played Barbie, Mary Kate and Ashley, and dress up. We also watched movies, because all that was on TV was the news.

The next day I went to my Mom's job. She was glad to see her friends. I made paintings and drew pictures. I walked around the office and saw everybody. It was fun and I did my normal stuff.

Then I went back to my friend Eve's house. We played computer games and then we watched a movie. It was called Peter Pan. It was good. We also played school. Sometimes I pretend to be the teacher and sometimes Eve pretends to be the teacher. Sometimes we pretend there is a volcano. It is really fun to play with Eve.

We get Eve's stuffed dog. We go to her parents' room. It has a big TV. One morning, me and Eve got the little TV. We watched Sabrina the Teenage Witch, and Full House. Then Eve's Mom came out. She watched TV with us.

Then we all went to the park. Eve brought her scooter and some jump ropes, and a smiley face ball. We went out to dinner.

One night Eve's family went out to their friend's house, so my family went to Dan and Fran's house. I went to Fran's studio. It is cool. She has paper mache balls that hang from string with different color paint on the bottom, and circle mirrors underneath it. She has paintings on the wall too.

My Mom and Dad went to my house to see if we could go back to live there. After three weeks, we moved back into my apartment. I was glad to be home!

Ellen Mullen is an 8 year old student at PS 234. She's not sure if she wants to be a writer when she is older, but she has been described by her former teacher as "an astute observer of the world." She will attend 3rd grade at PS 234 in Sept. 2002.

*On September 11*th

On September 11th
Ellen Mullen, age 8

September 11, 2001: A Poem

There lies a gap from which
It stood
A large façade of Brotherhood
Came tumbling down in our
Great Town
No trust, just hate,
You'll wear a frown
This building, was there
Is not
It's cold and ugly like a plot
This cannot be
Just look around for brothers
Are we
It took so long to grow
This tall
In one split second, began
It's fall
Build again, so tall and Free
A blessed site for you and me.

—*Barbara Simon*

Barbara Simon lives in Bayside, Queens.

A Nightlight For New York

by Mary Pflum

Nightlights for children are something of a hot button topic for pediatricians and child psychologists. Although some experts argue that the lights are helpful in easing a child's transition from infancy to "big kid" status by warding off the terrors of darkened bedrooms (and, in turn, the imaginary monsters that lurk beneath beds and behind closet doors)—others fret the lights are "needless crutches" that hinder emotional growth.

I'm a fan of the former group of eggheads—not the latter. And I'll go one step further. I'd argue that the occasional twinkling light in the dark of night isn't such a bad idea for grownups. Especially now. Especially in New York.

The city has been too dark—too scary—for too long. For six months after that fateful September day, Manhattan residents were forced to be brave in the face of darkness, on a number of levels. Plumes of smoke rose from the shattered remains of the World Trade Center by day.

But at night, there was nothing visible in lower Manhattan, nothing for the one-time sky gazers to admire. Nothing to fill the gaping hole the once-glowing, majestic towers left behind.

The chasm was palpable. A constant reminder of the all-too-real monsters our parents hadn't known to warn us about; the ones that continue to lurk in the shadows of a changing world.

The tried-and-true Empire State Building has done its utmost to lend some comfort to the city in the dark of night. After several nights of symbolic darkness, it glowed again—this time with red, white, and blue lights—to remind New Yorkers of the strength of their city, specifically, and of their nation, in general. But that was in midtown.

At the southern tip of Manhattan there remained a blanket of eerie, foreboding darkness where there had been none before. That changed on March 11th. When the sun set on New York on the six-month anniversary of the attacks, two mile-high beams of light—intended to be artistic replicas of the fallen towers—were switched on at Ground Zero. They're officially called a Tribute of Light. I like to call them New York's Night Light.

While a few cynics have lambasted the artistic display as costly or senseless or some combination thereof, I am among those who applauded and shed quiet tears of gratitude—and, yes, wonder—when they went on. The searchlights will remain in place—and aglow—for a few more nights, until mid-April. They are physical reminders that out of the darkness can come some light.

I gaze at them when I walk home at night from the subway station. They comfort me when I crawl into my bed, neatly situated beneath a window that faces southern Manhattan. "There," I often think to myself, gazing at the lower end of a city that's no longer so impenetrably dark. "That's more like it."

Like tots the world around, New Yorkers won't need a nightlight forever. Just for a spell—to help us complete the transition from scared children to brave soldiers. Just for long enough to let the monsters out there know they're not welcome here.

Mary Pflum is a television journalist who lives and works in Manhattan.

Bless You

by Mary Pflum

To those Americans out there who continue to subscribe to the notion that New York City has reverted to its "normal," former self, I submit the following, verifiable proof that the Big Apple is a city transformed: For the third time, in as many days, a New Yorker offered me a friendly—warm, I daresay—"Bless you," when I sneezed.

For those of you who grew up in a small town in America's heartland, as I did, taking the time out of your busy, or not so busy, day to offer a "Bless you" is commonplace. But not in New York City. Oh, no, the city that never sleeps known more for "Hey you," "Screw you," and the ever-popular "Fuck you!"

But not "bless you." Never!

Never in the "old days," that is. "Bless you" number one took place three nights ago. I was walking through the streets of midtown Manhattan at dusk, where my sneeze was heard and responded to by a brief-case-toting businessman. He actually raised his voice above the din of traffic to be sure it was heard, before he disappeared into the rush hour crowd.

"Bless you" number two was offered to me in an office building elevator—that closed space in which New Yorkers traditionally speak to strangers only to tell them to press a button, to move, or simply to get out.

This time, my sneeze was heard, and responded to, by a pair of corporate types, who interrupted their talk of the Yankees (among the most sacred topics of all New York conversations) and blessed me in unison.

And "bless you" number three happened in the unlikeliest of places: the subway, arguably the most impersonal New York setting, where people from every walk of life come together to ride beneath the city's streets—in silence. The twenty-something woman seated beside me, engrossed in a novel at the time of my sneeze, looked up, patted my arm, and offered me a reassuring "Bless you" before returning to her book.

To say that I was pleasantly stunned is a gross understatement—owing to all of my previous New York sneezing experiences in which my sniffles and "ah-choos" were either ignored or viewed as unwelcome, uncivilized interruptions.

This plethora of public "bless yous" from strangers in recent days is one more sign that the New York is undergoing a metamorphosis. Not the obvious altered skyline and heightened police presence on city streets, but something of a different kind.

As the days and weeks have unfolded since the attacks, it is true that a certain sense of normalcy has returned. Cars honk again. People yell. And everywhere, there's again that familiar sense of New York hustle and bustle.

But, two months after the attacks, there remains something changed. Once again, the Big Apple has managed to reinvent itself. This time, it's become a city of people who, while their guards are up all the higher—owing to fears of anthrax and falling skyscrapers—are willing to break down a wall, if only for a moment, to make the simplest of human connections.

To this new city, I humbly and gratefully return the salutation: Bless you, New York. Bless you.

Never Ending Sirens

Downtown, outside Da Silvano
Diners stop and stare
Motorcades of police, ambulances, trucks
Pass repeatedly through the night
Lights flashing and sirens wailing.

Downtown the sound of helicopters rattle windows
People in Tribeca show ID to pass police barricades
Stocking up on face masks to walk
Near the dusty, smoky, cloud to the south.

Downtown, New York's Jerusalem
Vivid reminder of happened just blocks away.

—*Jenna Fritsche*

Jenna Fritsche, a 13-year-old Tribeca resident wrote these poems in October 2001 as part of a 7th grade assignment for the NYC School for Collaborative Education.

I Don't Know...

Peaceful world, going to work, going to school
I don't know what happened, what's going on?
Confusion is in the air, screams cries, and smoke fill the sky
One big cloud
I don't know if people are okay.
My gas mask is clutched on my face
I don't know if I will be okay.
The Smell surrounds me,
it stinks and tastes grimy.
I don't know if my house is okay, I think
As I walk down Hudson Street
I am scared inside and out, will everything be all right?
I don't know if my life will ever be the same.

—*Jenna Fritsche*

Run

by Stephanie Izarek

I know what it is to run for my life—for my son's life and his future. For all that I loved, that I believed, that I needed, and never knew.

Walking East on Chambers, half a block from the routine September morning drop-off at PS 234—and half a minute toward an altered life. I know what it is to hear fear: the rushing, crushing roar; the obscenely muted pop. Clearly, the sound barrier has been broken.

Yes that's it, agrees the woman pushing the stroller. "Makes you proud to be an American," she says.

The day-long puzzle begins. "Oh my God! Oh my God!" Over and over again. The building. The hole. The fire. The hole. The death toll.

I know what it is to run. Run home. One block. One home. Run. My partner has yet to see it. I want my son.

My mother on the phone. "I am alright," I lie and stare West at the Hudson, and below at the school. I see the gaping mouths, wide eyes, tears, time—it all stands still. A man genuflects, blesses his breast in front of Gee Whiz. And the hot wind, sinister sound strikes again. My mother is my eyes, "Oh my God, another one!" I am the ears, and the touch, and the smell, and the fear. We are under attack.

I know what it is to be disconnected.

Another plane, another hole, an increasing death toll.

I want my son. I run. The elevator is not fast enough. My feet are not fast enough. My mind not fast enough. The stairs to the classroom, too high. The crying of children, parents, too loud. The fear, too palpable. The children's eyes. The children's eyes!

I know what it is to hold him. My boy thought I died. He clings to me. We run. Home.

I know what it is to stay. To wait. I don't want to stay. My home begins to shake and the fall begins. People run north, down on the street, screaming. My son starts crying, and I know we are going. Packing. Yes, packing. Pants for my son. His drawing. The teddy bear. The cats? Please, the cats. No. No time, no room. Run, as familiar life crumbles all around.

I know the surreal. The radios, the retellings already begun. People are lining the streets, in tears.

I know how guilt can consume you. Leaving everything behind, while saying all the while we are lucky to be alive. We run, leaving others behind to outrun glass and metal as it streams from the sky in one billowing ominous cloud that will forever follow in your mind, taking nothing less than as many lives as possible.

I know what it is to grieve, and disbelieve. To see a world change in an instant. And I know what it is to pray. For the answer, for the question, a reason, some meaning.

I know what is to fear. It is the landscape of my face, etched anew with astonishing haste, producing the map of my past before my very eyes. What does it matter, I wonder, now that everything has changed? My presumptions, assumptions, beliefs—stripped of every illusion, revealing nothing but a hollow murky place to dwell.

I know what it is to hate, to truly hate for the first time in my life. Clench my teeth, scream, repeat his sickening name, Osama. I know I must stop it cold.

And I know what it is to see grace and bravery. People risk their very lives, join hands with steely determination that some will be found alive.

I know what it is to ask for help, seek federal aid, wear hand-me-down clothes, share a friend's meal, and borrow toys for a little boy.

I know what it is to return. To come home, to remember a life I can no longer have. To be grateful for the chance, to run, if I want to.

I know community. I have seen people wipe away tears—they were mine.

Untitled

A Painting by Julie Rist

Point Thank You on Hero Highway

by Kate Walter

I watched summer turn to fall on the median of the West Side High-
way, where I stood waving my American flag, holding up handmade
thank you signs, saluting the rescue and recovery workers. The crews,
coming from long shifts, pass in their various vehicles—fire engines,
police cars, ambulances, motorcycles, army trucks, heavy rigs, MTA
buses, Verizon vans, sanitation trucks, Con Ed trucks, food and water
trucks—and they honk, blow sirens, wave back.

By the second week, a system had developed. Someone would yell
"Incoming!" and we'd rush to the downtown side. "Outgoing!" we'd
rush to the uptown side. The first few days it was so crowded; both
sides were lined thick with cheerleaders, so we didn't need the system.
After a few days, people went back to work, but since I teach at Man-
hattan Community College, which was commandeered in the clean-up
effort, this became my job.

The second Sunday after the attacks, two police cars stopped, and
the officers got out to greet us. This had not happened before. It was
the canine rescue unit from Knox County, Tennessee. The officers
wore green uniforms and had heavy southern accents. Two of them
removed their hard hats and asked us to sign them!

I wrote, "New York Loves You—Thanks." They took our pictures,
and we took theirs. The dogs Max and Chase jumped out to greet us,
too. According to the officers, the dogs were very stressed out and

needed attention. So everyone eagerly petted the hero dogs from Tennessee.

We asked the officers if they had ever been to New York before. "No, first time," one drawled.

"Ya'll come back," we said, as they sped off.

As our ranks thinned into a raggedly encampment at the corner of Christopher Street, it seemed important to maintain the vigil on this site, now dubbed Point Thank You on Hero Highway. I felt guilty if I missed a day. Although I never did an overnight shift, I was a regular on the highway for a month. We shared bottled water and Gatorade donated by the Red Cross. Most people were freelancers, retirees or the unemployed. As one woman explained, "I'm on the dole, this is how I'm earning money."

Our group included a few attractive 30-something women, who wore tight American flag tee shirts and Yankee caps. They flirted with some of the hunky cops and firemen. One officer from Buffalo, who stopped to snap our picture, insisted that a particularly sexy woman in a red tank top get into the forefront "for the boys back home." The WWII reference reminded me that we were entertaining the troops of this new war.

As the second and third weeks wore on, more personnel stopped to talk with us. A member of the FDNY handed out the now familiar posters of the three firemen raising the American flag at the site. A FEMA worker filled up with tears. Police officers from Fitchburg, New Hampshire, gave us special pins stating, "National Disaster Medical System." I fixed one on the collar of my jacket and felt recognized as part of this effort.

Police from Rhinebeck, New York, stopped to say goodbye on their last day before heading back upstate. One said, "The people of the city have been great. We wanted to thank you guys on the highway. Your support means a lot."

"Can you believe they are thanking us?" we asked each other.

On Sept 28, an official government car pulled up. A tall man emerged, wearing crisply pressed dark pants, a blue shirt, and a navy tie; two ID cards hung around his neck. He brought over a number of boxes and said, "These are gifts from the President of the United States. He wants you to have them."

At first I thought it was a joke. Then I realized it was not. He gave us boxes of M&M candy with the Presidential seal and blue stripes and white stars. "Thank you. What an honor," I managed to say, forgetting I am a liberal Democrat.

One Saturday, Police Commissioner Kerik stopped to thank us. "You're doing a great job, sir," I said, surprised at myself. I once called cops pigs.

Throughout the fourth week, state troopers and policeman from the NYPD and the New York Sheriffs office visited for longer periods. I wondered if the state trooper smiling at me was the same scary guy who gave me a ticket upstate or if he understood the pink triangle in the middle of my flag button. No matter. The cops hugged the women, shook hands heartily with the men.

For a month, I donned my New York Liberty cap and went to the highway religiously. I ask myself why I did this and why I kept coming back. The first week, I was caught up in the rush to do something. After a month, I realized cheering the workers was my way of coping. I didn't feel helpless; I felt needed. It was my therapy.

One officer told the story of driving back home at midnight on a rainy night. They were betting on whether anyone would be out on the median. "You guys were there," he said, "We couldn't believe it. You were there."

That kind of feedback helped keep the vigil alive. When I arrived for duty Saturday October 13, I saw that the West Side Highway was open to downtown traffic for the first time since Sept 11th. Two lanes of regular traffic and only a few rescue vehicles in one lane had altered the atmosphere. Now visitors from New Jersey and New York and Connecticut in flag-decorated cars were honking and waving at us.

"Welcome back to New York. Welcome back to the Village," I chanted, knowing it was time for me to break camp and leave the median.

I had done my duty and was needed back at my job at Manhattan Community College. Fiterman Hall, our new south building, is under the rubble and may have to be razed; my class now meets in a trailer on the West Side Highway, across from the pollution spewing operation where the wreckage is dumped from trucks onto barges in the river. I walk down Chambers Street past the carnage to teach in this depressing environment. My students have been great, and they keep me going. The dust flies all the time. My throat feels like I swallowed chalk. The college assures us the air is not toxic, but masks are available in the nurse's office.

Kate Walter is a is a freelance writer and essayist based in the West Village. Her work has appeared in many different publications, including The New York Times, NY Daily News, Newsday, New York Press, Yoga Journal, *and* The Advocate. *Kate has an M.A. in Media Studies from The New School and teaches Personal Essay writing at NYU.*

Harrison Street

We know what these are.
We know why they are here.
These are the derricks to load the barges
With the debris from the World Trade Center
To carry it away to the landfill
To be unloaded again.
Night and day for five months
The dump trucks have pulled up
With shovels, which are big enough to hold a pickup,
And released their yields.

I know what these are.
I know why they are here.
So I watch them when I can.
But for all this weight
My thoughts yield no words.

—*Elaine Kuperberg*

Elaine Kuperberg is a member of the staff of Borough of Manhattan Community College, from which she viewed the Harrison Street barges. She lives in lower Manhattan, where she attends "Grafitti" Baptist Church.

Homage

by Emily Moss

It was 6 A.M. I stood barefoot and shivering in front of my friends' flat-screen TV in San Francisco watching black smoke pour out of a monumental gash in the neck of the North Tower. My North Tower. The Tower that stood over my living space and life for 21 years—witness to my domesticity, peaceful and otherwise. It was my nightlight, my weathervane, and my compass.

My boyfriend and I moved into our loft on another blue-sky day in July 1980—he with his art supplies and quirky collection of suitcases; me with my assorted urban cowgirl outfits and great big speakers. In my youthful resistance to attachment, I accumulated only three photos in a four year relationship: one of us at the beach in winter, peering from beneath a shared coat; one at Niagara Falls, soaked in the nighttime rain; and another taken on a crisp billowy day from the Observation Deck of the World Trade Center, looking north to the whole of Manhattan, alone together on top of the world.

It was late afternoon when I first opened the door to my new apartment. I will never forget the thick bands of light coming through two enormous arched front windows, painting the wooden floorboards shimmery gold. In the very center of the empty floor sat a vase of fresh cut flowers of every color. And Peter, smiling, knew he had made a thing of beauty for me.

There have been so many flowers in so many vases since then, and almost as many boyfriends, though none so prized. The loft has since filled and refilled with chairs and sofas and tables and mirrors. And there have been animals, scuttling and sliding and rolling and resting, paws up, in the swathes of light on the floor. And there has been me, on the floor, with my lovers, among the furniture, losing buttons and beads and other less tangible things—under the silent watch of the North Tower.

Nearly every morning for 21 years, standing at my front window, I'd gaze abstractly at the North Tower, and in its solemn presence, align myself with the world. At the end of the day, no matter what transpired, those towers would be there. And every time I returned from points beyond New York City, the view of Manhattan, as it unfolded, took my breath away: the Citicorp building, saluting North; the bejeweled Chrysler and Empire State Buildings; and finally the towers, anchoring the island and pointing me home.

And so on the morning of September 11th, as I stood alone with the TV, my teeth chattering, holding myself, I saw a plane—the second plane—slice into the South Tower, erupt flames, and emerge as a fireball out the other side. I cried with the same depth as I had when Peter left (or, as said later, when I opened the door for him to go). I was folded chest to knee like a collapsible chair, crying with my hands covering my face, when little Hank shuffled in. He said, "This is bad? On the TV?" And Robin, uncertain how to protect both her son and me, said that yes, it was very bad what was on the TV. And so Hank, not three feet tall in his footed monster pajamas and holding his favorite *szord*, walked over and turned off the TV. "Okay. All gone. Okay?"

One week later, when I was able to return to New York, escorted by the police through the barricades and a singular darkness in the surrounding buildings to my home, I was nervous. The smell of burning electrical wires hung in the stairway and attached itself to me as I climbed the forty-five steps whose sags and dings and perilous turns I know by heart. The sight of the newly mute Loft, its coating of thick whitish powder broken only by some paw prints, was deadening.

Four months later, the view offers nothing but sky—no familiar ribbons of dull steel with perhaps a stole of fog, no checkerboard of lights as far up as the eye can see. My front window now fills with afternoon light—so much light that it is impossible to see through it, so bright that it is difficult to look at for more than a moment.

Emily Moss is an architect, who has lived in Tribeca for a very long time.

September 11th

I see
from my living room
a demolition site
tourists photographing
the destroyed architecture
the wrenching losses
the abysmal sadness
of what they think
are other people's lives.

I live here.

I saw the crashes,
molten flights
unimaginable then
even in the viewing
now
forever entombed in nightmare.

The ashes of hate, dominance,
desire, aspiration
fall on us
the survivors
the bereaved.

All the survivors.
All the bereaved.

And now
in a faith-shaking Biblical reversal…
we have the floodgates of Afghanistan

We have all that is Afghanistan.

by Linda Umans

Linda Umans is a retired public school teacher and resident of the Upper West Side. She volunteered in the recovery effort downtown.

Safe Horizon

by Linda Umans

I was at home on the Upper West Side when it happened, waiting for a delivery. I had the radio on, heard the first news and then sat glued to the television. It sounds far away, but it isn't. Homes are closer than you think in this city; the tragedies are closer still.

After the first shock, when I was able to think of *doing* something, I read about the help they needed at Bouley's Bakery preparing food for the rescue workers. I worked early morning shifts and when that ended, I found out through New York Cares that Safe Horizon needed volunteers as well. Safe Horizon had a temporary office on Chambers street where it would interview and process applications from displaced residents for financial aid.

I've always felt a special connection to the downtown area, especially the neighborhood close to Chambers Street. I have very fond memories of visiting my father when he worked as a diamond setter on John Street. This was back when Goldsmith Brothers, with their endless supply of wonderful papers and pens, was right there on Nassau Street. When he retired, people were just beginning to move into the lofts in his building, something quite unfathomable to him.

The person I most associate with this complex neighborhood is Reno, a comedian and performance artist. When I learned she had prepared a show at La Mama based on her experiences on September 11th, I went immediately. She was the only person I "knew" who lived down here. I often agree with her and when she finished performing, I felt that I was spoken for. If I were still teaching, my energy would have been concentrated on my students, finding ways to help them deal with all that happened. Maybe I would have been able to come here, too. As it was, I could only volunteer.

At the risk of sounding melodramatic, working downtown has meant everything to me. To deny this opportunity would have been tantamount to denying a best friend. I'm a native New Yorker, and I've often said, New York raised me. The work gave me an opportunity to do something direct and important...something I needed very much to do. I've met some admirable people, I've encountered extraordinary strength, and it has kept me connected to why I love this city.

As the months passed, I heard from some people downtown talk about how others are growing impatient with them. One woman told me how angry she gets when people tell her that it's "time to move on," which seems to be an easy thing to say these days.

Eight months after the 11th, there was an item in the *Times* about a group of volunteers who had helped families who had suffered losses in New Jersey. They threw a party celebrating "closure," no doubt fully expecting the families in attendance to respond to the "Are you ready to party?" call of the DJ.

Respect is difficult for some at these times. No question, it's harder to stay and really attend to the needs of those affected than to respond with other kinds of attention. You just might identify a little. That's hard and painful. But, it's allowing that kind of memory that often brings the comfort of understanding and connection to others and, often, to you, too.

A Chinese-American mother of a graduating high school senior told me about her great concern for her son. His bedroom windows looked out on the Towers and he was so proud of it that it was the first thing he showed friends when they visited. After the 11th, he keeps the curtains closed and is nervous about anyone coming into the apartment. He was never inclined to talk about himself and now, not surprisingly, he has become sullen and uncommunicative. He got accepted to Berkeley and wants to go as soon as possible. She started to cry, "I'm afraid he won't come back." She was afraid she had become part of the experience, part of a burned bridge.

An eighty-year old woman who was hospitalized several times as a result of a respiratory condition aggravated by the post-9/11 air told me of her fear of being alone. People were so nice at the beginning, she says, but now she is being forgotten. I met many people who were struggling to come to grips with the most fearful aspects of life, living in new worlds and making the bravest efforts.

Early on, I was interviewing a young, well-dressed man in the rooftop health club in one of the Battery Park City buildings. He was telling me about where he was when it happened and then, opening a large leather-bound file, gave me receipts for some of the material things he lost.

In the middle of this he paused, looked at me. He asked if I was a volunteer and I told him I was. "You came down here to help?" he asked and again I said yes. "I'll remember that," he said. So will I. I'm still here.

Rebuilding the Sphere

A photograph by Dan Costa

Identification

by Roger Wall

I didn't realize I had lost my driver's license until I approached the barricades on Houston Street. I began sifting through the loose cluster of cards in the zippered pouch that served as my wallet. A reader's card from the NYU library popped up. That seemed to be good enough. "Yeah, yeah, I saw it," the police officer waved me through.

I walked down Broadway shuffling the credit, bank, and membership cards in my wallet, hoping that my license had attached itself to one of them. All the stores, except for one, were shuttered. The light was beautiful. A police car barked its way past me. By the time I got to Canal, I gave up my search. The license was gone.

I told my story to the officer guarding the next set barricades. He listened patiently, then said, "I believe you, but I need to see some ID before I can let you through." I tried a pay phone—it was working—and called my girlfriend. Luckily she was home and could bring my passport and a utility bill.

Since buying an upstate house the previous spring, I had been having fantasies about not being a New Yorker. I took long weekends in our house on the dead-end road in a little village. In August I lugged work and computer upstate and spent two weeks working, hiking, swimming, and going to the local farmer's market. I started September often going up midweek just to mow the lawn.

I changed my voter's registration to vote in the town supervisor election for a slate of candidates opposing a resort development. I was also

77

thinking of changing my legal residence, registering my car and filing income tax upstate.

On September 11th, I was in the front yard, trimming grass in front of a stonewall. After my girlfriend phoned me with the news, I didn't return to my shears. I spent the day inside, listening to the radio (we don't have television) and sending e-mails—my own little command center. In the late afternoon I saw some neighbors, a brother and sister, in the street and went out to talk to them. They acknowledged me and continued their conversation. The man, who once owned our house, said, "I can't believe they postponed the election," referring to a state election. "That's just giving the terrorists what they want." His sister agreed. They talked about how the Catskills would be swamped next weekend because of the attacks. With mild disgust, the sister said, "Everybody is going to be coming up here next weekend." Then cheerful, because we're neighbors, "Are you guys going to come up?" I said I didn't know.

I couldn't join their conversation. They hadn't even asked about the safety of my girlfriend and son. I wasn't even sure where they were. The last time I had spoken to my girlfriend she was walking from midtown to Brooklyn to my son's school. Finally, the brother asked me where I lived in New York. I told him in the neighborhood beside the towers. He shook his head, and then commented on how the previous owner had done a fine job of repairing the shrub, a burning bush, at the foot of my driveway after a snowplow struck it.

I wasn't part of this life; I had to get out of there. Two days later, with passport and utility bill in my back pocket, I set out to replace my driver's license. I walked toward the Motor Vehicles bureau on Worth Street but as a cloud of smoke blew over me, a masked police officer at Broadway told me all the buildings east of us were closed. I walked north with irritated eyes, sneezing, to West 4th Street and headed to Penn Station to find another Motor Vehicles bureau. I exited the subway in the middle of a bomb scare and, sure that a second strike wouldn't come so soon, found the Herald Square office. When given the choice of reusing the photo on file or having a new one taken, I chose the latter. I wanted to remember this day. With temporary license between pages in my passport like a visa, I returned to West 4th Street.

I had nothing to do at home but wanted to be there and retraced my steps downtown. At Houston, then again at Canal I showed my temporary license, backed up by my passport. The officers scrutinized the temporary license. "Where on Hudson Street?" one of them asked. "Between Leonard and Worth," I said proudly.

The smoke was thick in the neighborhood, making the apartment stink. I watched from a window as residents walked up the street, pulling suitcases on wheels, handkerchiefs, scarves, and masks to their faces. I knew I would probably leave on the weekend to escape the bad air, too, but I wouldn't stay upstate. Downtown was in ruins. The mayoral election was coming up. I couldn't believe I had moved my voter registration upstate. What had I been thinking? New York is where I live. This is where I belonged.

Roger Wall is a freelance writer and editor who lives in Tribeca.

The Fall

Where has the Fall gone?
    Burning embers, but no leaves are falling.
    Sweaters not worn.
    Boxes unpacked.
    A sea of gray dust replaces the sea
    of leaves where children once played.

The Fallen are now the symbol of Fall.
    Papers, burned from years gone by litter
    my site and fill my senses—
    instead of trees turning red and yellow.

Clothes hang dusty waiting to be worn,
    but with only minutes to pull from the
    hangar—
    they will sit alone in the closet.

Painful thoughts of lights gone out
    instead of the cool evening air.
    There is no need for cooling air
    this Fall, but prayers for those who
    sit in the dark.

Cloudless blue sky as the building approaches
    for the last time.
    A clear sense of the impending season—
    for the last time as well.

One last memory of Fall as
    the PATH departs for the last time—
    no one knowing this train will not come back again.

Pain hangs heavy as plans disintegrate into
    the dust—
    into the depths below the ground.

Where has the Fall gone?
    It has passed by without any recognition.
    I dream of Fall—
    for cool walks through the Canyons, leisurely strolls
    along the Hudson.
    These—
    just dreams that stay tucked inside the
    roots of a tree that may grow again.

The Fall will once again become football games
    and picnics, Halloween and Thanksgiving.
    For some, the Fall will bring some pain
    for others it will symbolize the strength we never knew.

—*Kelly E. Colangelo*

Thoughts of the Neighborhood

There's a hole in my heart.
    One large hole pierced by
    two powerful beams of light.

    Never will it heal completely,
    leaving only one large scar.

There's an aching in my heart
    when it skips seven beats for
    the buildings I called home.

    Never will this aching cease
    until my heart should stop.

There's a heavy feeling in my heart,
    longing for seven pillars of strength
    and the activity of a thousand
    busy lives.

    Never will the longing cease,
    but time will help it fade.

There's a tear on my breast
    trying to soothe my injured heart.

The tears do not extinguish the lights,
but remind others of lights gone out.

Never will the tears cease, but
time will slow their frequency.

There's a ringing in my ear,
    reminding me of the silence—
The deafening silence of a busy
city on a weekday morning.

Never will the sound of silence
be forgotten, as long as I can hear.

There's a memory in my head.
    A memory sometimes too painful
to remember—
But too important to forget.

Never will I let anyone forget,
as I long as I'm alive.

—*Kelly E. Colangelo*

To My Family and Friends

(from an email written on September 12, 2001)

by Tracey Ceurvels

I know many of you have been leaving messages, trying to get in touch with me to see if I'm alive. I'm okay, as it were. It's not easy to make long distance calls. I had to press redial-I'm not exaggerating-thirty times to call my parents, thus I'm not returning calls.

As I write this, I hear loud sirens whizzing by my window. A caravan of trucks, dump trucks, bulldozers and cranes have been going by, a funeral procession on its way to the most horrific event this country has ever seen. Outside my building is a shrine, a FDNY engine, all of its windows broken and covered with debris, soot, pieces of the building, office papers, bottles, dust. Passers-by, crowds even, have been photographing this morsel of history all day and writing phrases like God Bless in the dust. One of my firefighter friends (for those who haven't been here, I live next to a fire station) told me their ladder truck had been demolished and this was what they had left.

Speaking of the firemen, it's not yet known how many are missing. I watched as some of the guys next door came back from "ground zero," as they called the site. I've never seen such long faces, such distant eyes. A couple of weeks ago one of firefighters was howling at the full moon just to be silly. Moments like those seem so innocent now, like that was before and this is now. I keep seeing familiar faces when I look out the window or go outside to the deli, but I'm still not sure if they're all accounted for, if they all made it back. I don't want to ask them either.

Early this morning, at 4 a.m., I woke to the thick scent of smoke, a burning smell that made my eyes and throat itchy. I had seen the murky smoke from my window when this all first happened, but couldn't smell anything. But the wind had changed and began blowing this blackness northward and into my apartment, which is only about 1/2 mile from the site. Far enough away but close enough, still.

On September 11th (911 as the firefighters pointed out to me), the day began as it usually does. I don't usually have the news on in the morning, but a morning program, *Good Day* I think, was on-a Martha Stewart-like woman talking about what to make for dinner, or something like that. I was eating Harmony cereal as I got ready for work. Then at 8:50 the news broke in, telling viewers that a plane had crashed into the World Trade Center. It seemed like just an accident at the time, so I thought I would go to work at my freelance job at the Federal Reserve Bank It is located just two blocks from the WTC. I took a shower and left.

I walked down East Broadway, the Towers on fire in full view, as though (yes it's become a cliché now) I were watching a movie. Everyone stared in disbelief. I turned on to the Bowery and continued for another block, against crowds that had been let out of work and were heading north. I continued south and a police barricade stopped me near the Metropolitan Correctional Facility. "Go north!" I told them I worked downtown. "Everything is closed, you have to walk north."

I walked about a block north, then stood with a crowd at the memorial for the Chinese-Americans who have served in a war, and watched a surreal scene: the two towers on fire in perfect view. I leaned against one of the memorial's stone columns, not quite sure what to do with myself.

Then the unimaginable occurred.

The south tower collapsed into a black cloud, something I have never and will never see again. Right in front of my eyes. It seemed unreal. A mere 1/4 mile away. People screamed, raced north. I gasped and said "Holy Shit!" aloud and began to cry. What an overwhelming, indescribable feeling. A man next to me asked, "What are we supposed to think?" My head was down.

I walked down Division Street, up Eldridge Street, then home to Canal, crying, a somber strange feeling I had never felt. When I arrived at my apartment the other tower collapsed. Two icons of this city, of this country, gone. People missing. People dead. The country turned upside down. It's like a war zone here. Fighter planes fly overhead. Police barricading Canal Street. You can't enter some neighborhoods unless you have proof that you live there.

As many know, Canal Street is usually crowded, with outside shops, restaurants, food vendors, traffic, congestion. Usually it's a headache to walk down this street, a maze of pushing and shoving. Last night when I walked westward on Canal, it was desolate, except for the police and the national guard protecting the streets. Mulberry Street in Little Italy had set up for the feast of San Genaro, which was to begin today. On other streets and avenues, blocks and blocks of trucks were lined up, waiting to clear away debris. Everything is in disarray. Nothing is normal anymore. I feel sick to my stomach.

Today I walked to a nearby supermarket where the army had set up their command post. A sight that doesn't look as though it could be down the street from my apartment. Past the supermarket, underneath the FDR were cars in complete ruin that had apparently been towed there from the scene. One looked as though it had been stabbed by a piece of the World Trade Center, as a piece of building was sticking straight out of the car. Another car was a burnt frame, some office papers strewn about what used to be the car's seats. I've seen a lot of office paper around, office manuals, faxes and such. I could keep writing but a part of me is speechless. Several months ago when I went to Italy, I originally wanted to visit Egypt. Many people advised against this. And now here is terrorism so close to home, literally.

On November 1st I'm moving to Brooklyn Heights, just across the street from the Promenade. I was looking forward to the panoramic view of downtown Manhattan, but this landscape has forever changed and so has much else.

Tracey Ceurvels is a freelance writer who lived in Chinatown for five years. She is at work on a collection of short stories titled, The Offerings We Make.

9/11/01 The Furies Unleash Themselves

The Furies unleash themselves
whirling dark clouds around
thick shoulders. Flying flames

are angry red, and
everywhere steel is melting
down to Ground Zero.

I have lost my talisman,
you gleaming towers so
silver, every single day in

morning sun. When I
look up, I see smoke
and emptiness. The loss.

We are patriotic now
and wave our flags. I have
seen two people, jump,

hand-in-hand from
a topmost floor. The one
thought in their heads,

now erased forever
more. Bidden and unbidden,
the Furies unleash,

and crash into the one
thought which is Love,
which dissolves evil. Forever more.

—*Dina Von Zweck*
(Copyright, Dina Von Zweck)

*Dina Von Zweck is the author of several children's books, a playwright,
and poet.*

WTC

Mornings I walk out and
look up, the World Trade Center
gleaming, sunlight from the east

streaming, buildings inoculated
with luminescent iridescence.

Even if it isn't so.

I flip through books at Borders,
decide what I want is
cappuccino, and ride the stainless

steel escalator to the Coffee Bar…
everything is metal, except the heart of words,
which are soft & fruitful.

Even if it isn't so.

Buying airplane tickets at the
Delta counter, a flight to Maui…
Paris…California…and to the
moon, moving slowly across the sky.

Even if it isn't so.

And a new Swatch battery, there's
a man at a counter, he'll pry open the back in a minute, he's still
there smiling at my fate tick-tocking away.

Even if it isn't so.

Duane Reade, I pick up my
prescription, here's the pharmacist
lady, an Indian beauty wearing
punky eyeglasses & Black Violet lipstick.
"Take two tablets, 1 hour before
your dental appointment." She smiles,
as if she'll always be dispensing mercy.

Even if it isn't so.

I buy a *New York Times* without
banner headlines, nothing
has happened today, except
a cow was born with 2 heads,
and the President cut brush on his ranch,

And the newsstand vendor asks
me if I want the winning LOTTO
ticket…a dollar & a dream…$20 million.

Even it isn't so.

There are smells I can't catch
on paper...pizza...cakes
and breads...flowers...the rubber of
heels as they head for PATH trains.
the sweat of men as they watch
stock quotes flash overhead.
fortunes are rising and everybody's
on time to meet their destiny.

Even if it isn't so.

They are slippery, those polished
floors...and the walkway to the
Wintergarden where palm trees
grow and grow and sparkle, all lit
with twisted lights. Nights...tonight
even...there a performance. Hundreds
hear a Swedish group, Garmarna, play
Hildegarde von B...and the sound of it
is still here, under rubble...burrowed
into bedrock...drilled into the center
of the earth like coins or cornstalks
or anything else of value. I'm
listening to everything I know
and love, the Twin Towers swaying
a tuning folk that tells the
truth about the way wind is blowing.

Underneath what "is" and what "isn't"
there lies a crispy burned place, the

red-hot core, two eyes that can
spot the mystery inside hate…and love.

Even if it isn't so…there's always hope,
screaming.

—*Dina Von Zweck*
(copyright, Diana Von Zweck)

Unbuilding

A photograph by Craig Hamrick

Momento

by Lisa Quattlebaum

Wednesday, 9/12

I'm at work and have just turned on the radio to listen to the latest news. The rescue team is searching for thousands of people—office workers, firefighters, and police officers, along with anyone who rushed into the building to help. So many people are lost, like going down in the Titanic and being buried at sea. I've changed the message on my company's answering machine to say that we are opened, returned the one message left, and although I am going through the motions of another day at work, everything seems so strange and unfamiliar. The catering event I coordinated for this Saturday has been cancelled—a wedding that has been postponed for a month. The groom said their family and friends, many of whom of whom were coming in from out of state and abroad are either stranded or were routed to other destinations. Others who were due to fly in this weekend have understandably cancelled their flights. As I think of how my plans for this coming Saturday have changed, I'm stunned by the frivolity of free time. It's difficult to think of planning for the weekend when the weekend will not come for many. My sense of time and space is disappearing.

Thursday, 9/13

I have just noticed that I've been wearing my watch for the first time in almost a year. I randomly chose to wear this past Tuesday and have continued to wear it, I guess on some subconscious level that I am now very conscious of. Work is trite, business is slow, and I am restless because I don't know what to do. It all seems so irrelevant, my wants and needs, all that I covet and indulge myself in; all the worries of life. I have managed to contact everyone I know in the city, by cell phone. I don't know anyone between the missing and the dead, but I've just found out that a colleague has a friend who she cannot get a hold of. What do you say to someone in that position? "I'm sorry" leaves too much empty space.

Went to the gym tonight. Am struggling with a kind of guilt for moving ahead, forward. I forgot about the fire and falling buildings for a split second. I fell into the trance with the music and I took such pleasure in the simple motion of my body. I think I smiled (I know I smiled inside), and then I looked up at the television monitors and caught eyes with the news anchor staring back at me. I looked down with embarrassment.

I am watching the news, and my heart is already broken. I live alone and my thoughts and emotions fill the apartment with a smothering thickness. They are still searching for people, and my mind is filled with crazy scenarios of people, huddled, grabbing on to life here; there may be nothing but darkness. Their fear must be tremendous. How do they hang on? How would I?

Friday, 9/14

Watched Larry King last night and was struck by an interview he had with a downtown looking young women with a four-year old child perched on her lap. They were at a candlelight vigil at Union Square (the sobbing mouth of what they call Lower Manhattan.) The woman said, "Violence doesn't stop violence." As grade school as it sounds, I can't find an argument against it.

Have posted signs at work about volunteers and donations needed. I plan to volunteer tomorrow. There were bomb threats at Grand Central and Penn Station. Bush advises us to continue on with life and our regular routines—re-establish a sense of normalcy in the midst of what has happened. Easier said than done.

Saturday, 9/15

The morning was quiet and strange. Lazy lounging felt inappropriate. I cleaned the apartment and did laundry. Ate only an apple and a piece of cheese—have lost my appetite. They didn't need more volunteers—over 300 people showed up at 8am to help. They made sandwiches for the Ground Zero rescue teams, doctors, and aids, organized boxes of donated clothing, boots, socks, hard hats, flash lights, batteries, water, hope.

On the way to the gym, my only salvation, I passed police on the corners, and a Red Cross truck casually made a turn down Broadway. The massive billboard advertising HBO's "Band of Brothers" seemed more like a premonition than a preview. Perhaps, I am being dramatic, but everything from the police and bomb threats and the posters of missing men and women posted outside my gym (lives that barely brushed against mine) to flags flying EVERYWHERE is so loaded with meaning, and at the same time it's all meaningless; they can't bring back the dead. The symbolism changes: one minute, sorrow and fear, the next, unity and support, ultimately war.

Sunday, 9/16

Stopped by work to check up on the business, say hello, use the bathroom, and so on. Began chatting up a storm with the semi-new waitress who I have barely said more than Hi and Bye to. Another case of lives just barely brushing against each other. I thought I was friendlier. It turns out, she lives—or used to live—two blocks from the WTC. She was evacuated from her apartment with all of the other tenants that morning and has yet to return. She has been shuffling between her friends' and family's homes, and is spent. We talked about a lot of things: the WTC attack, the missing and likely dead, what used to be, and all that is yet to come.

Monday, 9/17

Got an email from a German couple whose wedding I planned over a year ago. They sent warm hugs and sympathetic words. They also sent the best news I heard in weeks: They have a new baby girl, Elena. I have never been so excited about a newborn. Elena is like the best karmic kick in the butt the universe could send—LIFE. Showed everyone at the office. Took it as a sign, and held it up like Norma Rae for anyone interested to see.

Spoke to waitress M, tonight. She was crying in the stairwell, not able to summon the energy to be angry at her homelessness and utter emotional, psychological displacement. We hid in the bathroom, and I asked her if she wanted to talk, keep crying, hit something, or swear. She asked me to tell her some good news. I paused, struggling to think of something. Nada. Hum. Finally, I said, "You woke up this morning."

Today, no one else was found alive.

Lisa Quattlebaum is an artist and writer by night, and an event planner by day.

Home

by Molly Mokros

On a late night last December, my father raised his water glass in the air and said to me, "Here's to New York feeling like home."

The word home. Say it. The word home starts by exhaling a breath of air and ends with a hum on the lips. The word home isn't usually capitalized, but it could be. The word home is comfy and easy and nice. The word home sounds and feels like, well, home.

After my father's impromptu toast, we went back to hanging picture frames and putting dimmers on the lights in my Manhattan apartment, which I had lived in for nearly five months. All the while the word home-suddenly breathless and unspeakable—floated in my mouth. My father's use of it struck me as strange, not because New York did not feel like home, but because it did. Here I was, standing in the middle of a room imagining what the walls might look like painted yellow. Painted walls, after all, signified permanence.

At what moment did each of the thousands upon thousands of people who moved to the city call it home? How many times did they have to say it before it didn't feel like a lie or something of which they were trying to convince themselves? When did the word hum on their lips so naturally they didn't notice? One woman I know told me she knew New York was home the day she unpacked her suitcases-which was six months after she had moved to the city.

And for me, at what moment did Ohio simply become Ohio and New York become home, as in Home?

I had moved to New York City only six weeks before the terrorist attacks of Sept. 11th. During those weeks I was homesick for Ohio-a gold and green dream that lingered with me, wide-awake in the stark gray angles of the city. I ran every morning along the pier at Riverside Park keeping my eye on the George Washington Bridge. It was a twinkling exit. The way home. Lush Ohio lay somewhere just on the other side.

On Sept. 11th, the city and I were not yet a good fit. Within hours after the attacks, I rented a car and fled to my small hometown, where I was sure the world would seem a normal place to be again. As I crossed the George Washington Bridge, I looked over my shoulder at the black cloud. I shuttered. I turned forward. Straight-ahead. Home-bound. Lucky.

That night my father took me outside and pointed to the clear Ohio sky. Not one plane flew. "Pray to God," he said, "that you never see such emptiness, hear such quietness again in your lifetime."

Ohio was solemn. My parents were solemn. The next morning as I sat with them talking at breakfast, we used words like bomb and survivors over cornflakes and coffee. The news was on in the other room. New York on Sept.11th had turned into a buzz in the ear coming from faceless voices.

I wanted to tell my parents that it was not the same. I wanted to tell them that the news could not make them feel the warm air on their skin as if they had walked along roadway the morning of the attacks. The news could not tell them what it felt like to walk on the Upper West Side alongside a thousand expressionless faces. How eerily beautiful the day had been.

On Sept. 15, I was a bridesmaid at my best friend's wedding. We wore silver dresses. We posed for photographs on a sunlit golf course. We held our champagne glasses in the air and toasted the newlyweds in what felt to me to be a momentary suspension of disbelief. In this silver circle 400 miles away from a pile of shattered glass and steel, we still believed that certain things were invincible. Our warm wishes for the couple floated in the benign, dustless air.

Right after dinner the music started. I stood still on the dance floor. Right then, a woman came over to me, expressionless. She too was in from New York, a graduate student at New York University just like myself. She had also been in the city on the day of the attacks and had returned to Ohio for the wedding. We excused ourselves from the celebration and found a quiet corner.

I told her how hard it was to smile for all the photographs. I told her how ridiculous I felt in silver. How my mother assured me the celebration would make me feel better. The woman told me how she felt too guilty to eat the last few days. How she was tired of explaining why. She told me how she could still smell the fire and dust in her hair.

I left my best friend's wedding early. Ohio suddenly seemed a little less golden. I had to get back to New York. The next day, I drove east on I-80 and somewhere in my mind Ohio shrunk to just the tiniest pinprick of light.

As I carried my bags up the stairs to my apartment, I felt relieved. There was not one silver circle of make-believe to excuse myself from. Grief was not a little voice coming from another room. I was with people as quietly miserable as myself. I was Home.

Molly Mokros is a graduate student at New York University.

A Remembrance

by Regina Gordon

Slowly, as we emerge from the nightmare of September 11th, the mourning goes on for those who lost loved ones and friends, for the brave souls, who gave their lives to save others, for all those missing and not recovered. We mourn the lives and homes destroyed for the innocent children, for the lost sense of safety we all once enjoyed.

A vibrant heart of our neighborhood has been destroyed. It had virtues. It was a gathering place, a site of entertainment, a place to look out on the world from its great heights, to sample chocolates and eat ice cream with funky names, to buy tickets cheaply to a Broadway show—or even for a trip around the world—to feast by eye and taste the colorful offerings of local farmers, to admire art by Miro and Calder, among others, to nestle into a chair with a book or listen to an author discuss his work, to enjoy a sumptuous meal or a drink from on high as the lights of the city twinkled below, and so much more.

The soaring towers may not have been lauded by architecture critics, but their significance to our neighborhood and to New York was evident. When approaching the city from any direction the towers loomed large as a beacon and for those in the vicinity, meant home.

The World Trade Center served as a gateway to the glorious glass-enclosed Winter Garden, with its majestic palms, and site of music and dance, and the World Financial Center and Battery Park City (built on landfill from the WTC excavation), the lovely gardens, much-used parks, and public art sculpture. At the edge of all this is the Esplanade with bustling activity and views of the harbor and Lady Liberty welcoming and watching over us. These sites remain and will again be accessible to us. Over time as we heal from this tragedy, there will remain a glowing memory of something that was bright and beautiful in our piece of the world.

Regina F. Gordon is the managing editor of The Southbridge Sentinel.

Empty Sky

Black smoke from the building is blooming
Flames the towers are consuming
What other tragedies over us loom?
I try to peer through the sickening gloom.
And now I look up at the empty sky—
Ashes of disaster are floating by
What next? Who can tell?
This is Hell

by Anne Moy

Lucky

by Sharon Lew Block

My good friends know how much I have loved my neighborhood. Battery Park City is an enigma in New York City. It is a small town in a big city. Many people who have lived in NYC their whole lives, don't know how to get there. You still always have to tell the cab driver where to turn off West Street. No one knows there is a great new school there, or the most amazing park. It's been a growing secret here, and it's a working mom's dream place.

In the last three days I have gone from hysterical, to sad, to angry to completely confused. I have decided to write this, because my husband purged himself in a letter to his friends, and I have decided to do the same. It might seem self-indulgent, but so be it. I think it's important for people to hear the stories of the people this catastrophe has affected. My heart aches for those families who have lost loved ones. My story has a happier ending and I feel guilty for that. I feel so bad for feeling sorry for myself today.

Our neighborhood was The World Trade Centers, The World Financial Center and all the buildings connected. It's the mall we shop in, it's where my shoe repair place is, it's near where my grocery store is, and our drug store. All the babysitters meet there inside, with the kids in the winter. My daughter knows some of the store workers, especially at The Gap, by name. We go there to take the subway, everyday and every night. All those places are gone now.

So many families were separated and had a very hard, traumatic time trying to find each other, trying to find out if their loved ones were okay. There must have been something like 5,000-8,000 people forced from their homes in Battery Park City alone. That is the size of most suburban towns. There is debris, body parts and pieces of buildings all over the place. And of course, we are the lucky ones.

My morning began by taking Emma to school. It was an amazingly beautiful day and we both commented about the bright sun. I remember talking to a bunch of Mom's outside the school about whether or not we were going to enroll our kids in Hebrew School, and where we were going for Services. All the mom's were saying we should stay in the city; so all the kids could be together for the holidays. I was running late, so I know by the time I got out of the school building on Warren St. and The West Side Highway it was about 8:45a.m.

I had not crossed the street yet, when I heard a plane. I actually made a joke to myself like—what are we being bombed or something? I looked up and the sun was in my eyes, so I never saw the plane actually enter the building. All I saw was the huge explosion, all I heard was the loudest noise ever. The earth shook, everything stood still for a moment. I dropped to my knees. I was hysterical. I thought a bomb was dropped and the plane kept going because I never saw it go thru the other side. I ran in a circle for a moment I think. I was cursing my cell phone because it wasn't working. I was shaking. A total stranger and myself were shaking and crying and hugging each other. I don't think we said a word to each other. We were in the middle of the highway.

Like in a chase seen in a movie; all the cars on the highway and Chambers St screeched to a halt. Everyone was looking up and screaming and crying. One of my neighbors ran up to me I think she was in shock, She was screaming "I saw that, I saw the whole thing" It was literally right over our heads.

I remember running back to Emma's school. All I could think of was to get Emma and Sage near me. I was frantic. I arrived in the building. Most people didn't get it. They thought it was an accident, but then someone came screaming inside, who had seen the whole thing. I had to explain to people that I was pretty sure this was no accident. It was a terrorist act. Two moms' became hysterical when I told them what I thought. It had never even dawned on me that it might be an accident. After that we were all hysterical and in line for the pay phone to call our husbands, 20 hysterical moms.

That's when the second plane came, the sound and explosion shook the building. Much like an earthquake. More mom's came running into the school; they were still outside looking at the insane sight of the first building with a hole in it. The neighborhood was being bombed. The enormity of being bombed twice in five minutes, right across the street from us, was more than you can imagine. It meant they could just keep going.

That's it. I run up the stairs to Emma's classroom I am talking to myself, "get Emma, get Emma, and don't stop." I get to her classroom; many parents tell me I should stay put, stay calm and don't go outside. I can't. I have to be outside. I have to go find Steven and Sage. And I absolutely must be holding my Emma. I thank everyone for his or her advice, the teacher makes me take a deep breath, and reminds me not to panic, for Emma's sake, and I know she's right. I deep breathe and say, "Now bring Emma to me." She's already scared. Her classroom faces The World Trade Center. They heard the explosions in class. They are 6-years-old.

We run outside toward the river, away from The World Trade Center. We see another classmate with her mom up ahead. We run up to them, so Emma has a buddy. We are all relieved to not be alone. The girls are visibly scared. We decide to wait in the park. We thought it would be calmer and safer there, but then these police helicopters came flying in. They landed in the middle of a very small park. Right in front of us. Everyone is freaked out. More loud noises, SWAT Team type guys come running out of the helicopters. Now, I'm even more scared. Nowhere is it safe and calm. I need to get Sage and Steven.

I start walking with Emma back toward our apartment building. We are walking south along the river promenade. The World Trade

Centers are huge; we see them everyday, they looked bigger than ever before. There is an open view from the promenade that is indescribable. I see someone fall from the top of the first building, and then I see someone walking throw up right near me. I see people waiving white flags to come and get rescued. The buildings to me are just a sea of people, who are stranded. I tell Emma not to look up, which only makes her look up more. I just needed to see Steven and Sage and know they are okay.

I knew going back down there was probably not the best thing to do. I can't sleep now, thinking about what I put Emma through by walking back down there.

We finally arrive at our building but we are not allowed in. We are not allowed near the entrance of our building and our street has been closed off. I start asking strangers to use their phone. I finally get to use a fax line phone from one of our neighboring buildings on the side street. I finally get through to our house for the first time, but they are not there. I leave a crazy message on the machine. Now I'm hysterical again. We are standing outside, the other women I am with does reach her husband. He was home; he said he's coming right down to get them. She actually apologized to me for her good news in finding him. I started crying. A man came running by with a transistor radio, and starts screaming, "The Pentagon was just bombed." We all look at each other in absolute distress.

No one knew what to do. At that moment the earth started shaking again, the noise was loud, but different then all the other loud noises. People started screaming, "we're getting bombed again." We didn't know yet, but that's when the first building fell. We looked up and this huge black and gray mass of debris and smoke came at us.

"Run" was all anyone screamed. I was worried we weren't going to make it. I really thought there was no way we could run faster than this stuff was attacking us. I was worried Emma would be trampled. I don't even remember how we actually got to Battery Park. I just remember we were there, and I saw someone get on a bus. A man waived at me to bring Emma, It turned out to be an abandoned bus, and the driver fled leaving the keys inside. He must have thought he was going to die in that bus. So did I.

I was worried about Emma being able to breathe. What is in this dust? We are spitting it out, and breathing into our clothes. I thought she might suffocate. We get on the bus and huddle up.

Then the second building fell. It was not as loud cause we were further away now, but the wind dropped the debris and smoke right over us. It was like thick black snow, with big chunks in it. It was eerie outside. Thank god for that bus. The EMS and Fire trucks started screeching around, their drivers screaming. "Move this fucking bus, now." A young guy, I think around 20, had been sitting in the front seat. He turned around and said, "I am taking this bus out of here, and going as far uptown as possible." We all just stared at him in silence.

We drove past the South Street Seaport, which was covered in thick debris. Some people got out at the Brooklyn Bridge, I thought about it, but I wasn't sure. A man screamed at me to stay seated, there might be a bomb on the bridge. I knew I didn't want to go to far from our neighborhood because I needed to find Sage. I started crying on the bus, telling the driver I needed to get out at 23rd St, near my office. I couldn't go further than that. I was hysterical at the thought of leaving Steven and Sage behind. He wasn't going to stop, but I begged him to let us out at the 23rd street exit on the FDR. We got out, people wished us well, and a man took off his shirt and threw it to me, so Emma could breathe into it.

Emma and I walked off the entrance ramp; people were walking along the FDR from downtown, because all the trains were out. A few people came to help Emma get over the fence that separates where the cars should be. Emma comments on how nice everyone is. She is acting like a Stepford-child. She is in a zone, and I realize this right then.

When we get to 3rd Avenue, I realize people are looking at us funny. I am a zombie. We are covered with dust; we look like refugees. We are refugees. In Gramercy everyone acts like nothing happened.

Kids are in the park; the whole world was different uptown. People are breathing differently. The sun is shining again up there. There's no smoke, no chaos. I break down again at Park Avenue. I look downtown and see the smoke and start praying out loud for Steven and Sage and Della, our babysitter. A stranger asks me if I just lost someone, and I say, "I'm not sure." I didn't even know if Sage was with Steven or Della. I didn't know if Steven had left for work, and went to the subway. I didn't know if Della took a walk to the Greenmarket at the World Trade Center. I was definitely thinking the worst.

All Emma talks about is how thirsty and itchy she is. Her shoes hurt, she has been walking a lot. I buy her water. Everyone in the store is staring at us, but none say a word. They were afraid to ask I guess. We finally make it to my office building.

I'm afraid to get in the elevator, but I do. I walk in, and Caryn tells me Steven, Sage and Della are there. Steven comes over to me and I break down. It never dawned on me for one minute they might be there. I wail. I never knew I could cry like that. Like the cries you see old women do at funerals. I've never been like that. I wailed. Loud.

Steven had heard the first explosion and ran downstairs to get Della and Sage who had been on their way to the Greenmarket. It exploded right above them too. Della had grabbed Sage out of the stroller and ran her back to our building. They all ran to Emma's school, but we all missed each other there, probably by just minutes. They ended up running uptown until they reached my office. Not knowing where we were. Steven is a wreck.

Now we are all very jumpy. Loud noises freak us all out. I think planes overhead will forever scare me. We need to find a new home quickly. None of us could live there again. I don't even want to go home to pack. Emma's school is closed, and being used as a triage center for all the victims and workers. I need my babysitter, so I can go back to work. But I don't even know where we are going to be staying. I don't know yet how traumatized my daughter is. And I think she needs to see her classmates to share their stories. Too bad we can't call any of them. Our next few weeks will be crazy. But we are all together and safe, and won't be leaving each other's sides for a while.

It's odd for us to keep hearing people say things like "it's business as usual, uptown" many people are like "yeah, life has to go on." I know in a sense this is true, but we can't even sleep yet. We close our eyes, and see all these horrible images of the morning. Our community is gone. Our neighbors are gone. Our park, our post office, our churches and temples, our school, for now and our homes. How does everyone just move on? All downtown people are traumatized for a long time to come. There are so many victims of this act. The world will never be business as usual for any of us, anywhere. And I have a need to make sure everyone understands that.

But today I will hold my kids and my husband close, and thank god for how lucky we are.

Sharon Lew Block lives in New York City. This account was written on 9/15/01.

Sorry

I'm Sorry

Riding by on my bicycle on the way to work, I see
Everyone wanting to be heard, over THE LOUD AIRPLANE NOISE

Neighbor, understand, please, we can work our differences out, here
on the street, in front of our home, WHAT USED TO BE OUR
HOME (My son, daughter, husband, wife, you see, was there,
know my pain,
hear me
see how EVERYTHING IS DIFFERENT
under this naked sky)

I'M SORRY! CAN YOU HEAR ME?

We are talking about the everyday,
But it is the once in a lifetime my words don't reach

strangers and neighbors, husbands and wives,
coming together and a part

I struggle to find peace within myself,
as my country looks for peace
in desert caves

Turning the corner, it is silent,
only pain can be heard here,
floating on a gentle wind

This winter morning heated
by fires that won't go out

Be well, friend

—*Beth Wachter*

Beth Wachter is a publisher of educational print and video materials and has lived and worked in downtown Manhattan for 15 years.

Yesterday I Wanted To Go To France

fiction by Tracey Ceurvels

Today I'm in the mood to go to China, but since I can't exactly skip school and get on a plane I'll ask my friend Marcy if she wants to head down to Chinatown. She likes the turtles that some storeowners sell along with fake designer watches and sunglasses. Me, I like the coconuts. Every time I get off the train on Canal Street, I buy one. They crack a hole into it so you can drink the milk straight from the nut. We also go into this small Buddhist temple on Mott Street, where we light incense and pray. This is how religion should be, not the Sunday services my mother drags me to, more than ever lately since a friend of hers died.

But yesterday I wanted to go to France. After what happened just a month ago on September 11th, I want to be anywhere but New York City. What I've done since that day is read cookbooks of places I want to visit, making some of the recipes for my mother and me. My mother thinks I'm crazy. She hates that I hate her cooking. I told her that I get tired of chicken twelve different ways and dried out pork chops with macaroni and cheese.

"Fiona, I work hard all day to put dinner on the table for you," she tells me. "And you don't appreciate it."

After dinner my mom always confesses that she's never heard of half of what I make, but that she does like most of what I prepare. Last week I was obsessed with Indonesia, since in history class we were discussing when Indonesia gained its independence from Holland. Every night for a week I cooked Indonesian food. One night I made peanut chips, beef rendang and jasmine rice that I cooked with pineapples. My mother said it was a bit too spicy for her. That she was up going to the bathroom all night since she'd had to drink so much water.

But yesterday I wanted to go to France. After school I went to Barnes and Noble with my friends. They went straight to Harry Potter books while I went to look at the cookbooks. I came across this great book "Parisian Home Cooking" by an American guy who just upped and moved to France. After school I told my mother that that's what I want to do when I graduate.

"Mom, we can get an apartment near the Sorbonne. I'll go to college there and every night I'll cook dinner."

"Fiona, I told you. We're not leaving our rent-controlled apartment to go anywhere. Now just be happy with where you are."

"But Mom. I'll make steak au poivre with frites and flourless chocolate cake. I'll go to the markets like Michael did and buy fresh produce. It'll be incredible."

"Who the heck is Michael and what are frites?"

"Michael is the guy I just told you about. He's a chef who moved to France and wrote this amazing cookbook. And frites are french fries, but I'm sure they taste much better in Paris."

"Fiona, why don't you focus on your homework, and stop reading all these cookbooks?"

After she said that I ran into my room, yelling, "Fine. I won't cook for you anymore!"

This is how my life has been progressing lately. After school or after dinner, me running into my room, yelling something at my mother. She drives me crazy this woman who always says she gave birth to me.

My mother is a waitress at the diner on 11th and Broadway that Seinfeld made famous. She serves burgers, fries and egg creams all day to old people in the neighborhood and the tourists who constantly ask questions about Seinfeld, Elaine, George and Kramer. My mother has never even seen an episode of Seinfeld, yet the customers expect that she knows every detail. They ask her where the Soup Nazi is, and they crack jokes that they think she's never heard, like "What time is Jerry stopping by? I need to have a word with him." This bothers her, but she covers her annoyance and the usual diner gruffness with a fake smile that makes the old timers who sit in her section leave twenty percent tips.

My mother works the 7 a.m. until 3 p.m. shift five days during the week, which means that I get ready for school alone in the morning. That's when I blast music and sing. No, I don't like pop music. I can't stand Britney Spears who all the boys in my class drool over. Call me a weirdo but I love singing along to the opera *La Bohème*, which I first heard during music class at school. My high school is close to the diner, but I never go in there to visit my mom. I hate diner food anyway—pancakes, cheeseburgers, disgusting tuna melts. I can make that stuff with my eyes closed. But why would I even want to?

Early in the morning, mom walks ten blocks north to the diner and then ten blocks back home. She doesn't stray much from this route, doesn't stop in somewhere for a cup of coffee, or enter a store where she might have seen a shirt she likes in the window. No, my mother is always home at precisely 3:15 on the dot. I'm not usually at home after school. I hang out with my friends. Like I said, we go to the bookstore, or to a coffee shop where we do our homework. Sometimes we go watch some of the boys we like play basketball. We're not bad, like some of our classmates who go off and smoke pot behind St. John the Divine. I guess they figure that the NYPD would never bust them at a cathedral, or that God would save them. Who knows what they think, but I know I want my brain cells. When I'm a famous chef, I'm going to have to memorize a lot of recipes.

But a few times I have been home when mom comes in at exactly 3:15, and I say, "Mom, take another route! Sit on a bench and feed the birds. Buy a new hat. Go to a matinee. Find something to do in the afternoons other than watch Oprah and her self-help topics." But she gets mad at me, tells me to mind my own business, then I go into my room and sit on my bed for hours, planning menus for my future job as a chef.

My bedroom is frilly as though a baby lives there. My mom says she can't afford to redecorate my room so I still have pink lacy curtains and a comforter decorated with cartoons of a princess in her many ball gowns. On my bulletin board I have pictures of me and my friends. Some are from our modern dance recital last spring. Some are of us being silly in Central Park during the summer, the first and only time I went roller blading. I nearly fell into a couple walking their baby near Strawberry Fields because I didn't know how to stop. The father yelled at me and since then I haven't roller bladed. There's one picture of my dad and me. It's of us on the carousel in the park. I'm wearing a really ugly plaid dress, my hair is in pigtails and my dad is wearing sunglasses and smiling into the camera at my mom. I also still have a doll that my parents gave me for my sixth birthday, the last birthday we were a family. Its clothes are very worn and it's missing an arm but I can't seem to throw it away, so it sits on the bed with my cookbooks and my notebooks filled with recipes cut out from food magazines.

I feel bad for my mother. My dad died when I was six, around ten years ago, and she's been alone ever since, except for a few dates with some guys who came into the diner and asked her out. One guy wanted to marry mom after the second date, but she said no and was I glad about that because I thought he smelled like Lindenberger cheese, which, if you've never smelled it, is disgusting. Another guy was twice her age. I actually liked him, because he took me to see Annie and Diary of Ann Frank on Broadway. But she thought he was too old and dumped him when he showed up at the diner with two dozen red roses.

My friends tell me that my mom is pretty. I really can't tell, because to me she's just my mother. She's a lot younger than my friends' parents who all look ancient to me. Mom wears the same size jeans, she's told me, that she wore before she had me and her hair is still long and blonde and sometimes men in the street whistle at her. My hair is long and blonde, too, but being a little chubby, I don't get the whistles which is fine with me. My mother looks so young that strangers sometimes think we're sisters. My father "swooped her up" as she always says over a game of pool at a downtown bar, when she was only twenty. Then they had me right away. Since he died in a car accident on the New England Thruway while he was on his way to a baseball game in Massachusetts, the only time I've seen her happy is when she was planning her first trip back home to England. I try to leave her alone and not bother her too much, because I know she still misses my dad even though she'd never admit to it after ten years, but yesterday, when she told me to stop reading cookbooks, I was furious.

When I ran into my room I got in bed and wrote in my journal: *One more year until graduation. How will I make it?*

Graduation will be at the end of June next year, so I've decided that July 1st I will take off to Paris, which means that I need to start saving my twenty dollar a week allowance, and maybe get a job this summer. That means no more caramel Frappuccinos from Starbucks. Those drinks are delicious! I'm addicted but I'd rather save so I can sip *café au lait* at Laduree or Brasserie Lipp—places I've read about in *Gourmet* magazine.

I'll miss my cat, Chloe, but I still want to leave. Maybe I can take her with me. I don't care if my mother doesn't come with me. She can stay in New York and serve bitter decaffeinated coffee and rubbery hot dogs to Seinfeld fans for the rest of her life.

After writing a few more pages in my journal, mom called my name from the kitchen where she had just hung up the phone, said that the firemen down the block had invited us for dinner. She's been spending time down there, lighting candles and saying prayers with the nuns.

"I don't know about this, Mom," I said. "Won't that be weird? Having dinner with a bunch of firemen?"

"Fiona, they need our company right now. They just went through an awful time. Now get dressed. We'll walk over in twenty minutes."

The firemen had prepared angel hair pasta with grilled shrimp. I never realized they made such good food at the firehouse. We sat at a long table in their kitchen. I loved their kitchen: a big stove with eight burners and an enormous refrigerator filled with lots of meat and vegetables that one of the firemen told me they buy at Fairway. While the men were finishing the meal, I walked around the fire trucks parked inside. The trucks were shiny now, all the debris had been washed off weeks earlier, one of the men told me. Boots, ready to be jumped into, stood next to the trucks. Photographs, collages, flowers lined a wall. It was unbelievably sad and I could have cried as I looked at photographs showing the sons and daughters of the missing, but I composed myself. During dinner, no one mentioned "the incident" as my mother calls what happened on the 11th. Everyone, I think, was still in shock at the loss. It was kind of cool to eat there, but I was secretly hoping that the alarm would ring and they'd have to run out because I didn't know what to talk about. I kind of felt like I was invading someone's funeral, only this one was for much more than one person.

My mom brought brownies for dessert that she topped with candied red fire hats. She can be real corny sometimes. One of the firemen told her they thought it was cute. While we ate the brownies, one of the firemen asked me how I liked school. I told him it was fine, but I dreaded the next year until I graduated and could move to France. I also told him that there were no cooking classes at my school, like I heard they had in the old days, which bummed me out. I heard they used to call cooking class Home Economics.

"Strange name, don't you think?" I asked.

"Yes, sure is. I guess cooking is your thing?" the fireman David said.

"Yes. I want to be a chef. I'm moving to France to learn cooking techniques from some of the famous chefs. Then I'll come back to New York one day and work in one of those four star restaurants downtown."

"Can't your mother teach you about cooking? These brownies are pretty tasty."

"To tell you the truth, those brownies probably came from a box—Duncan Hines or Betty Crocker. No, my mother doesn't cook the way I'd like her to. She makes the same old meals, over and over. Me, I want to learn about emulsions, reductions, how to make confit."

"Where did you learn all these terms?"

"From cookbooks, *Bon Appetit* magazine, some of cooking shows on the Food Network."

"Hey, I watch the Food Network, too. All the firemen make fun of me. Which program is your favorite?"

"I love Molto Mario," I told David. "He's the best."

"I do, too," said David. "The way Mario talks about Italy makes me want to book a trip to Italy. Maybe I'll take my wife there one day."

"Yeah, I want to go to Italy, too. And I've always wanted to eat at Mario's restaurant, Babbo, which is in the Village. My mother won't take me. She told me she can make spaghetti and meatballs just the same, but I told her she didn't understand Italian food."

"When you graduate maybe she'll take you to Babbo. You know, before you move away from her."

"Maybe. Anyway, thanks for dinner. I loved the homemade garlic bread."

"You're welcome. Stop by anytime. And when you come back from France, I hope you'll cook for us."

"Yeah, but that's going to be a while. I still have over a year before I can leave."

Just before we left the firehouse, mom said goodbye to one of the firemen, Eric, the one who had done most of the cooking. This wasn't a friendly *I'm your neighbor* kind of goodbye. Eric put his arm around my mom and she smiled like a bride walking down the aisle for the first time.

"I'll pick you up at the diner when you get off work tomorrow," I heard him whisper to her so that the whole crew wouldn't know his plans for the next day. "We'll go to the movie you want to see—*A Beautiful Mind.*"

"I can't wait," she said, giggling as though she were being asked to the prom. "I haven't been to the movies in years."

I said goodbye to all the firemen then Eric walked us outside, where candles were still flickering and flower arrangement were beginning to wilt. Then Eric kissed my mom. I couldn't believe it. In all these years I never saw my mom making out. I started walking home ahead of her, then she caught up with me. We didn't speak the length of the block to our apartment building. She went into the deli to buy some cigarettes while I went upstairs.

We live on the upper west side in a fifth floor elevator building, but I always take the stairs so I don't have to make small talk with the elevator guy. Up in our apartment, I sat in my room circling recipes from a Madhur Jaffrey cookbook I want to make for my graduation party. (I know it's a year away, but this is going to be one special day.) I want to have an Indian theme to my party, all those breads, chutneys, and curries. Maybe I'll dress up in a sari. I saw a beautiful one in a store window on Lexington and 27th. But then I wondered who will like this Indian food that I make—my mother certainly won't—and who will even be coming to my graduation except my mother, a few of her friends from the diner and my aunt and uncle who live upstate. All my friends will be at their own graduation parties. I put the cookbook next to my bed and decided to plan my party another time.

I heard the key in the lock of the door. Mom was home from the deli. I smelled smoke from her cigarette, which she claims only to smoke on her morning walk to work. I put on my headphones since I'm not allowed to play loud music and thought about how those firemen looked at dinner. They smiled and entertained us as best they could, but you could tell they were hiding their feelings. They looked lost. They'd invited my mother and me and seemed to enjoy our company. But God, what can you possibly say to these grown-ups who just lost most of their friends? *Sorry* just didn't sound right when it first came out, so I avoided the topic. I thought about what David, one of the firemen, had said to me before we left the firehouse.

"When you move to Paris and become a famous chef, don't forget about us. And don't worry about your mother. When you're gone we'll be sure to invite her over for dinner more often so she doesn't have to eat alone."

I decided that for lunch the next day I would stop by the diner, sit in my mom's section and order a grilled cheese sandwich.

Tracey Ceurvels currently lives in Brooklyn, N.Y.

Awakening

by Dan Costa

It was a beautiful summer morning and I stayed in bed. I don't do it often, but it is one of the great benefits of working from home, antidote to the fear and uncertainty of freelancing. When Stef left with Emmet for school, I was happy in the still, quiet apartment. I could not know the fall was coming.

The sound was louder than a car crash, sharper than a clap of thunder, and very, very close. The only echo was the sound of people screaming. I can see Emmet's school across the street. The building looked fine, but there were people running in the schoolyard. I heard a man's low, loud voice shout, "Get the kids inside! Get them in the building." I knew a plane had crashed, but the school looked fine. In my mind, I thought it must be in the nearby baseball field; that was the nearest open space.

Stef met me by the elevators. She had dropped Emmet off, but hadn't reached the subway yet. Together we went to the roof and saw the hole in the tower. Together we ran across the street to get our son out of school. I wanted to take all of the children, but I couldn't. We went back to the apartment.

This was the first of many mistakes I would make that day. I said we should stay in our apartment, safe from falling debris and away from whatever catastrophe was to hit next. It seemed like the smart move. Even as a crowd formed eight floors below watching the fires, watching people in the towers, watching them fall. We couldn't see the towers, just the people on the street. Emmet wanted to know why the crowd kept gasping and crying out. The fire, I told him, the fire.

We stayed there until the first tower fell. The rumbling shook our building like an earthquake. I thought it was too late, that my error had been fatal for my family. No time to pack. We took the stairs. Eight floors. At some point I picked up Emmet. I didn't put him down for ten blocks.

There was no dust cloud when we got out of the building. WTC 7, which fell later in the day, shielded us from the debris. I ran by people on the street all watching the towers. I didn't tell them to run. They might get in my way. They might get in my son's way.

Emmet kept telling me the towers were falling and I kept telling him they weren't. I really didn't think they would fall. After the south tower fell, I started doing the math. How many blocks are 110 stories? I kept running. I kept telling him they were not going to fall.

As I ran North, Emmet faced South, toward the towers. I asked him not to watch, but couldn't prevent it. People were jumping. I don't know what he saw.

There were lines 10 people-deep at the pay phones. Almost everyone was crying. Cars were stopped at the side of the road with people gathered round listening to the radios, with the smoking image of the North Tower behind us. We heard that the Pentagon had been hit. We were among a flood of people walking north. There were no cars, just the sound of distant sirens heading south. At times the crowd would panic, start to run, and then slow down. We were a herd, scared and on the run.

We had just made it to Houston Street when a cry went out; I turned and watched the second tower fall. I thought of keeping Emmet from watching it, but it was too late.

"What about the people?" he asked. The people got out I told him.

"I told you it would fall," he said. "You were wrong." He repeated this for months.

Crossing Houston we were passed by a woman in tears, screaming, "Those bastards! Those bastards." Her hatred hit me like a wave. I was in shock, filled with a sense of vulnerability and helplessness. I wanted to know whom she was talking about. She shouldn't assume it was Arabs or Islamic radicals. Islam has many faces and most of them are peaceful and tolerant.

She never said it was Arabs.

In the Village, I found an ATM machine, withdrew $500, and thought about where to go. Our friend Julie lives on 8th Street, so we went there—a place we would become very familiar with in the coming weeks, thanks to her generosity. It was there we started to plan our escape from the city.

Hide

We were out of our apartment for two months. We divided our time between Stef's ex-husband's house and chic downtown hotels that offered discounts to displaced residents.

Stef's ex-husband, Rob, lived in Tarrytown, NY, at the base of the Tappan Zee Bridge. It was difficult for me, and I imagine, harder for him, but it was the best thing for Emmet. He lost one home, but simply went to his "country house." Rob stayed at his girlfriend's apartment, while I slept in his bed with his ex-wife and son. His generosity is the biggest reason Emmet has faired as well as he has and I will be eternally grateful for it.

When we needed to work, we stayed in New York in hotels. With few tourists or business travelers, most of the hotels in the city had rooms at a discount. We stayed downtown, at the Tribeca Grand, which was among the most generous. For weeks, we tried to gain access to our apartment to get clothes and belongings, ferrying Emmet across town to a temporary school.

The room we stayed in was gorgeous. Stainless steel bathroom counters, Kiehl shampoo in the shower, and spring water that cost $14 a bottle. The center of the hotel is open and filled with banks of candles, like a cathedral. The halls are dark and the windows admit little natural light. Amber lights covered by metal grills light the halls. It was like an air-conditioned, *Architectural Digest* version of hell.

The management and staff were welcoming and understanding. In addition to renting us a $400 room for $100, they said nothing when rambunctious children played on the fine leather furniture on the lobby. They even created a children's menu for kids who didn't go for Roasted Loin of Venison or Peppercorn Crusted Wild Scottish Salmon. Aside from the fact we were three to a bed, it was a very fashionable dislocation. We didn't even have to make our bed.

Still, it remained a boutique hotel. The staff was gorgeous, well groomed, and invariably dressed entirely in black. The doormen seemed oblivious to the toxic air and dust that constantly blew up Church Street. I wonder if the management would let them wear gas masks, perhaps black ones? DKNY?

Eventually, we were forced to check out of the $100 a night Tribeca Grand and into the $200 a night SoHo Grand. As I understand it, there are more models working at this hotel and the extra cash is used to keep them unfed.

We were a block from Canal Street, which is covered with large metal slabs. When cars crossed over them, it created a low, loud, and sometimes, shocking rumble. It happened all night and each time I wondered if the world—or at least my small, densely populated part of it—was coming to an end.

Given our apartment's proximity to the "pile," we started looking for a new apartment. We found a small two bedroom that was still in the neighborhood, but several blocks North. Even though Tribeca was a disaster area, it was still in high demand. The landlord wouldn't come down from $3500/month. We were turned down. It was the first sign that things would go back to normal.

Return

Our building was covered in rubble, window blinds, parts of the towers, and parts of the people who worked there. The air was a mix of burning materials and the dead for weeks, but it did get better depending on the direction of the wind. In late November, we were allowed back.

A company that specialized in removing toxic materials had cleaned our building top to bottom. We were told all of the cleaners were certified to handle hazardous materials certification and they moved through the building vacuuming, mopping, purifying. Everything we owned was removed, wiped down, and bagged. Seventy five percent of them spoke only Spanish and the rest were from Kansas. One of them carved a small cross into my teak desk with the words "God Bless."

Because our windows were closed, we didn't have much dust but we still threw out all exposed, curtains, pillows and bedding. At night we would see people combing through the furniture and curtains and taking things away. This city recycles. We bought air filters for every room to recycle the air.

From our living room, we can watch planes approach and land at Newark airport. At night, putting Emmet to bed, I can watch planes, so low, fly up the Hudson. One every 17 seconds, on weeknights. I can hear their engines through the window.

I hear the end coming. I hear it every day. At night it is worse. I hear it in the sirens of police cars. I hear it in the screeching of tires. I hear it in the hysterical cries of children. I hear it in the distant roar of jet engines. I get up, look out the window, and wait. Sometimes I turn on the TV to make sure they are just showing commercials.

Of course, if you can hear it coming then there is nothing to fear. A plane moving at 563 MPH hits very quickly. It is like lightening, if you hear it coming it isn't coming for you. Still, once on you have been struck, the sound of thunder is never the same.

Post-traumatic stress affects every decision I make. I can't leave home without a cell phone. I am addicted to the news. I avoid walking near parked vans. When any news report begins I check if the anchor is smiling. If they are smiling then nothing terrible or life threatening is happening. At least three times in the last year I have been absolutely sure I was going to die in the next 60 seconds. For the cleanup workers the stress has been even worse.

The construction workers and fire fighters that scoured the site for weeks had it far harder. Although the buckets of body parts lasted only a few days, they collected remains through the winter.

During the winter, I overheard two workers talking at Kitchenette. It was 10am and they were having their dinner as I had my breakfast. They were talking about how hard it was to work seven days a week for months on end. They concluded that after 8-weeks they would be burnt out. "It is just so hard, you know, taking things a part," one of them said. "The word is construction, not destruction."

Cope

A lot of these men and women spent their off hours at bars like Reade Street. This was the first place I wanted to go after the 11th. Surely I, along with the rest of Manhattan, needed a drink. A Columbia University study found that drinking and drug use had increased after 9/11, in New York and D.C. I would guess there had been an increase of sadness, depression, anger, fear, respiratory ailments, and spontaneous crying as well.

The bar opened a week after the attack. Most of the other restaurants were closed much longer. With this many construction workers, firemen, and cops in the neighborhood the bar would probably have been opened with or without the permission of management.

I would have liked to spend more time there after the attacks. To listen to the stories of the guys working on the pile, buy them beers, and perhaps even tell them my own. But when your family is terrified and you can't focus to complete an hours worth of work it is hard to justify bar time. I have made my stops, but they have been few and far between.

In the bathroom there is satellite photo of the site torn from a newspaper. It puts a sad spin on taking a pee, letting you relieve yourself without any real relief. It fills you with sorrow when you empty your bladder. This is the way most of the country see the site, from space, simply the absence of buildings. From the ground you can see the jagged edges.

Tourists who come here to get close to the pile don't see it any clearer. They stroll their infants down Greenwich Street and hold them up above the fences to get a better view. I watched a young girl with her boyfriend as they took turns having their pictures taken in front of the pile. She smiled wide and arched her hip, as if she had just climbed a mountain. I wanted to scream at them, but I just stared at them with disgust.

There is a globe on the bar at Reade Street with a big hole where central Asia used to be. It was an angry, stupid gesture but I wish I had done it. I have never been and entirely gentle spirit, but I have never felt hate like this. Maybe it is because my sense of injustice is tainted with genuine fear.

We know who did this. A man living across the globe leading an organization of militants wanted to kill as many Americans as they could, capture the attention of the world, and sow fear in our hearts. The plan was implemented with terrible efficiency. We know who and we know why. And yet explaining this to my seven year old is beyond me. Wanting to kill thousands of people you have never met is a little worse than just being bad.

And yet, that is what I want now. There are men across the globe that I have never met that I want dead. I take some solace in the fact they struck first. It is really a form of self-defense, but this rings a little hollow. I feel the hatred within me and it makes me sick.

With thousands of us dead, how can we not blame them? Hate them. Less than a week after the 11th, I hailed a cab in front of Grand Central with my girlfriend. The first cab to pull up had a driver with turban, probably a Sikh and as far removed from Al Queda as your average Morman. Behind him was a cab with a black driver. Without breaking stride we entered the second cab. This is not me.

My high school history teacher would be appalled at my action. Mr. Bresnahan, "Bres," was as good a Liberal as he was a teacher—smart, passionate and if you forgot you homework, or just weren't working as hard as you could, a real son-of-a-bitch. When I was 14, he brought the entire class to Boston to protest the state speed limit increase to 65 miles per hour. He said it was bad for the environment and would increase highway fatalities, and he was right. Of course, none of us were old enough to drive. It was just an elementary exercise in self-rule, in giving a damn.

Bres died on September 11th. He was many miles away from the towers, in Western Massachusetts where I grew up. His illness has nothing to do with terrorist attacks, but the timing made it seem like a personal attack on his life, his dreams, his country. I have to remind myself that he survived other wars, so did his dreams and his country.

Hope

I have never loved New York more than now. And it isn't for any reason other than those intangible moments that make life worth living. I am not out finding cool new bands, rubbing shoulders with the cultural elite, or even making inflated New York City money. I have been having beers at Reade Street with an accountant that does the books for St. Paul's, learning about soccer from my Romanian doorman, and drinking coffee served by an 18-year-old girl that left her son in Trinidad to be raised by her mother.

Emmet got a toy building set a few months after the attacks. It was a medieval castle structure called, I kid you not, the The Twin Towers. He spent days building it up and tearing it down. Sometimes he even used a toy plane. I tried to get him to play something else, maybe some thing more constructive. He told me not to worry. He says these towers are far in the future when there are no rescue workers—just super heroes who "will save everyone."

By June 2002 just about everything that was the World Trade Center is gone. Everyone has a plan for what should be built there; some plans are quite beautiful others just look like giant office parks. Replacing office space won't replace what was there.

We renewed our lease for two years, and yet I still don't know that whether we should stay or go. It is the same question we had that terrible morning in September. I just know I want to stay, I want to build something, and that has to be enough.

Dan Costa is a freelance writer and editor and a five-year resident of Tribeca.

Shadows and Light

A photograph by Dan Costa

I Miss My Stars

by Laura Leston

You can't see stars in the city sky. On some clear nights, you may catch the celestial glow of a planet, like Mars, Venus, or Jupiter—but no stars. But for me in Tribeca, the night sky outside my window was filled with stars: twinkling in the windows of the World Trade Center Towers.

Growing up, I spent nearly every summer and winter holiday here, watching the towers grow themselves, noting their progress as a parent would their child's. Each trip, my brother and I would have a contest to guess how many stories there would be. But like Brigadoon, the cityscape appeared and disappeared as we drove closer, so we could never really count. I suppose that's why I chose to live within view of them when I moved to New York.

The towers were familiar and comforting to me. And what they lacked in architectural beauty, they made up for with multiple dimensions, angles, and views. For nearly 20 years, I watched the towers change in character, depending on the time of day, the season, and the weather. They would sparkle as they reflected the morning sun, glow golden with the setting sun, or mysteriously disappear behind a heavy fog. "The World Trade Center is missing," we would laugh. "Who stole the towers?" On stormy nights, I watched lightning dance off the North Tower antenna.

On that cloudless Tuesday morning, the Towers seemed a bit unreal; like an all-too-perfect retouched postcard photo. Suddenly, these static and usually stoic monoliths became animated with frightening new personalities. The postcard became like another tourist souvenir: a shaken snow globe, but this time with a flurry of flying glass, metal, and office paper. And then, one tower after the other melted like sandcastles beneath a wave. Clouds of ash and glass chased us like some demon serpent, winding its way through the streets of lower Manhattan. Those horrible new personalities imbued by the evil minds of men rather than the daily rhythms of nature will haunt our dreams forever.

The terrorists viewed them as temples dedicated to greed and godlessness. We knew them as marvels of American engineering and ingenuity. To some, they were the welcome gates to New York, America, and the promise of a better life. To most New Yorkers, they were simple: A practical place, a workspace for earning a living, our daily bread.

What used to be is irreplaceable, and I do miss my stars. Whatever comes next, it must be a memorial to those who were lost, but also a monument to those who remain and to New York, the real survivor—battered and bruised, but still standing. There must be towers, the tallest structures in the world and a new grand portal to New York, and on each, thousands of lights—one for each soul lost that day. I would wish upon them every night.

Laura Leston has lived, worked, and loved Tribeca for 20 years.

United We Stand

United We Stand
Emmet Izarek Smith, Age 8
(pencil on paper, April 2002)

About the Editors

Stephanie Izarek has been a writer and editor for 13 years and a resident of Tribeca for 9 years. She lives downtown with her eight-year-old son, Emmet, and her partner, Dan Costa. She is currently the Executive Editor of Scholastic's *Parent & Child* magazine.

Dan Costa is a freelance writer and editor who covers technology and culture. He has contributed to *PC Magazine, Computer Shopper, Fortune/CNET Technology Review, Time Out New York* and other publications. He is currently working on a cookbook.

0-595-24368-1

Printed in the United States
879700003BA

9 780595 243686